Paul's SAT®
Advanced Writing

Paul Kim

Paul Academy

Paul's **SAT**®
Advanced Writing

Paul Academy

Welcome to Paul's SAT Advanced Writing.

Welcome to Paul's SAT Advanced Writing.

If you're here, you are already somewhat familiar with the New SAT Writing section.

44 questions. 35 minutes. 50% grammar, 50% reading. You've heard these before.

You consider yourself a *proper grammarian*. Differentiating *who* and *whom* does not phase you in the slightest. Subject-verb agreement is like child's play. You know your comparatives better than you know the back of your hands. Modifiers never dangle.

Great.

Your practice exam scores are not *bad*. You are likely getting fewer than 3 questions per passage and better on good days. However, it just never seems quite possible to get that elusive perfect score. It's always *those questions*. You know, *those questions* you just can't study for.

If this sounds like you, take heart, because this book was written for you.

This book is designed to tackle the four most difficult question types in the Writing and Language section of the New SAT. (And yes, you can study for them.)

Sentence Combination
Transition Words
Addition/Deletion/Placement
Diction

Each section consists of a quick guide, followed by practice questions.

The best way to approach the practice questions is to do them little by little. Try not to binge-solve a whole section of Sentence Combination questions. Instead, savor the questions, as if you're tasting artisanal olives. I recommend you work on all sections simultaneously. Go slow, and resolve to work on a few pages every day.

The College Board (CB) likes to emphasize that the Writing section is about *the everyday*. You can glean from this philosophy that CB considers mastery of English as something like how *well you wield the language as a tool*.

Let's say you are an apprentice blacksmith, working to become a renowned master. The mastery of your tool—the hammer—comes not just from *reading about* the hammer; doing that will just yield *theoretical knowledge*. It must be complemented by *practical knowledge*. This bulk of the work has to be *your experience* of using the hammer.

We want to strike a good balance here and help you every step of the way.

Godspeed!

Paul Kim

CONTENTS

Chapter 1

Addition/Deletion/Placement

Chapter Guide

Addition/Deletion/Placement

1. Read the question first!
2. Reduce the numbered sentences to their logical functions. (**Paraphrase**)
3. Look for keywords or key phrases.
   - Articles (a, the)
   - Transition words
   - Pronouns (it, this, they, them)
   - Chronological order
4. Bracket closely related ideas.

[1] Richard Dawkins, the evolutionary scientist, coined the term "meme" in 1976. [2] In his book, *The Selfish Gene*, Dawkins compared the transmission of biological information through genes to that of cultural ideas. [3] He noted that just as DNAs do, ideas proliferate through imitation, replication, and retention. [4] The picture inspires a hoard of imitators, they replicate the original with slight modifications. [5] For instance, a funny cat picture with a clever caption catches attention of the masses. [6] At this point, the funny cat pictures become an identifiable entity within the culture, commanding and retaining influence.

In order to make the paragraph most logical, sentence 5 should be

A) placed where it is now.
B) placed before sentence 1.
C) **placed after sentence 3.**
D) DELETED from the paragraph.

Unlike other types of questions on SAT writing, it's beneficial to read the question first. How do you know when to do this? Easy. When you see numbered sentences in the passage, scan for the placement question, make a note of the relevant sentence. In this case, we are interested in sentence 5.

As you read the paragraph, reduce each sentence to its function within the paragraph.

Sentence [1] introduces the topic. Dawkins and meme.
Sentence [2] elaborates on the topic. Dawkins wrote a book.
Sentence [3] discusses findings. Book says ideas and DNAs transmit in a similar fashion.
Sentence [4] introduces "the picture." Wait, what picture?
Sentence [5] introduces "for instance" and "a picture." A picture starts to get popular.
Sentence [6] discusses consequence. "The pictures" become identifiable.

Addition/Deletion

1. Summarize the paragraph in terms of Topic, Scope, and Main Point.
2. Do not read Yes/No or Kept/Deleted
3. Play True/False with the sentences. Eliminate false choices.
4. Play Necessary/Unnecessary with the remaining choices.

Picking the correct choice will result in a clear, concise paragraph that stays within topic and scope.

You have probably seen questions that look like these:

At this point, the writer is considering adding the following sentence. Should the writer make this addition here?

At this point, the writer is considering deleting the underlined sentence. Should the sentence be kept or deleted?

You will be given two choices (Yes/No or Kept/Deleted) with corresponding reasons.

These questions test you on your ability to understand the paragraph's **topic, scope, and main point.** When you see these questions, stop. Don't solely rely on the underlined section for the answer. You must read the **paragraph** and summarize it.

Example 1:

Some scientists are uncomfortable with examining bits and pieces of culture through a biological lens. Critics of memetics argue that the field is essentially a pseudoscience so long as it cannot produce empirically supported research. Thankfully, advances in neuroimaging promises empirical data in the near future.**1** "The idea of a meme is itself an evolving concept," Hopkins notes jovially. "We're going to have to see how it mutates over time."

At this point, the writer is considering adding the following sentence.

The journal *Evolutionary Neuroscience* reports that it is now possible to quantify and provide numerical representations of the way human brains process ideas through imitation, replication, and retention.

Should the writer make this addition here?
A) Yes, because it adds a relevant research finding from a scientific journal.
B) Yes, because it elaborates on the claim made in the previous sentence by citing an authority in a relevant field.
C) No, because it undermines the main point of the paragraph.
D) No, because it is not relevant to the paragraph's discussion of empirically supported research.

The paragraph's **topic** is "empirically supported research." The **scope** is to discuss the scientists' criticism. Without data, the discipline is bunk. The **main point** is that "advances in neuroimaging" can solve the problem that the scientists cite.

Now, tackle the prompt, and **play True or False with the choices without reading "yes" or "no."**

Keep (A), because it is true. It's not the answer yet, though.
Keep (B), because it's also true. The prompt elaborates on the "promise empirical data."
Eliminate (C), because it's false. Providing the possibility of empirical data does not undermine the main point.

Eliminate (D), because it's false. "Numerical representations" explains "empirical data" and is therefore relevant.

On easy questions, it will be possible to eliminate three choices based on the true or false test. On difficult questions, you'll be able to narrow down to two. Next, consider **necessity to paragraph**. Pay special attention to the verbs used. Should we add the sentence because it "adds" something? Or, should we add the sentence because it "elaborates?" While (A) is true, the fact it adds a relevant research is not the reason why it should be added. We should add sentences to **advance** the point made in the paragraph, and an elaboration performs that role. The answer should be **(B).**

Chapter 1

Addition/Deletion/Placement

Practice Questions

Criminologists are using increasingly sophisticated methods to aid investigative work. One such revolutionary method is DNA testing. By analyzing the DNA footprints at the scene of crime, forensic scientists are able to provide compelling evidence at the molecular level. **1** Since no two persons—save for identical twins—share the exact DNA, such evidence boasts unmatched accuracy.

1

At this point, the author is considering adding the following sentence.

Small human droppings like hair and skin cells can help scientists learn more about the role of DNA and the intricacies of its structure.

Should the writer make this addition here?

A) Yes, because it adds an important detail about the importance of DNA.

B) Yes, because it supports the paragraph's main point about the study of the DNA.

C) No, because DNA is not important in the field of criminology.

D) No, because it is not related to the main point of the paragraph.

[1] With a built-in movie camera, today's smartphones can turn its user into a potential content creator. [2] These days, however, any aspiring media sweetheart can point and tap: all that is needed is originality. [3] On an online platform like Facebook live, a person can look into a smartphone and start broadcasting. [4] In the past, appearing on screen in front of a home audience was practically an impossibility. [5] If you wanted to be on TV, you needed to dedicate your life and career for the pursuit.

2

To make this paragraph most logical, sentence 2 should be placed

A) where it is now.

B) before sentence 1.

C) after sentence 4.

D) after sentence 5.

The term "Renaissance man" refers to a person with a wide range of pursuits, from physical strength to poetic sensibilities. The epitome of a Renaissance man was undoubtedly Leonardo da Vinci. Although da Vinci is best known for his artwork such as The Mona Lisa and The Last Supper, he was also a curious natural scientist, an eccentric innovator, and a wise philosopher. He dissected human cadavers to teach himself physiology. He designed a flying machine (which never flew, sadly). **3** <u>He was born out of wedlock and did not receive much education.</u> He once declared, "Simplicity is the ultimate sophistication."

3

The writer is considering deleting the underlined sentence. Should the sentence be kept or deleted?

A) Kept, because it introduces the quote in the next sentence.

B) Kept, because it explains why da Vinci was able to become a Renaissance man.

C) Deleted, because it blurs the focus of the paragraph with a loosely related detail about da Vinci.

D) Deleted, repeats information that has been provided earlier in the paragraph.

Trendy diets like South Beach or Paleo only serve to exacerbate the yo-yo effect, a vicious trap for those who are trying to lose weight. Media presents these fads as quick, miraculous solutions to serious problems of lifestyle and habit. **4** A simple traditional rule of "eat less and move more" is discarded in favor of exaggerated pseudoscience.

4

At this point, the writer is considering adding the following sentence.

Trendy diets not only attract overweight women but also overweight men.

Should the writer make this addition?

A) Yes, because it reinforces the argument presented earlier in the paragraph.

B) Yes, because it describes a potential benefit of trendy diets.

C) No, because it undermines the main point of the paragraph.

D) No, because it blurs the focus of the paragraph by introducing a loosely related detail.

[1] One restaurant in Palo Alto, CA is bringing the principle of transparency to fine dining. [2] True, the food is quite pricey, but the owner guarantees quality and honesty with every order. [3] The costs of all ingredients are shared online for any patron to see. [4] The menu prices fluctuate to reflect the costs, and the owner is quick to provide reasonable explanations for any changes in the prices of the dishes, which typically range from $40 to $70. [5] "It's always better to be up front with the prices. After all, we want to bring the best for our customers, so it is only fair we charge for it," he says. **5**

5

To make this paragraph most logical, sentence 2 should be placed

A) where it is now.

B) before sentence 1.

C) after sentence 3.

D) after sentence 4.

[1] The meteoric rise of the Internet in the past decade has had a devastating effect on what used to be the American way of consumption-shopping at retail stores. [2] Gone are the days of strolling down the shopping mall aisles. [3] People no longer line up for Black Fridays and prefer to get their shopping done online on Cyber Monday. [4] This development indicates a grim future for companies already invested in the retail business. **6**

6

To make this paragraph most logical, sentence 3 should be

A) placed where it is now.

B) placed before sentence 1.

C) placed after sentence 4.

D) DELETED from the paragraph.

For a long time, art lovers have speculated about the identity of the woman depicted in The Mona Lisa, Leonardo da Vinci's masterpiece. A new report suggests that the woman, whose mysterious smile has enchanted so many, was likely the wife of a wealthy Florentine merchant. **7** Before the age of photographs, posing for a portrait was not a luxury afforded to the poor. Only the wealthy, like an Italian merchant, could afford to sit for hours, if not days, to "get the picture taken."

7 ▬▬▬▬▬▬▬▬▬▬▬▬▬

The writer is considering deleting the underlined sentence. Should the sentence be kept or deleted?

A) Kept, because it reinforces the main claim made in the paragraph.

B) Kept, because it provides an important statistic that is explored further in the next sentence.

C) Deleted, because it repeats information that has been provided earlier in the paragraph.

D) Deleted, because it blurs the paragraph's focus on the identity of the woman in Mona Lisa.

[1] Take Louis Armstrong, the father of modern American pop music, who revolutionized Jazz. [2] Working with Fletcher Henderson's orchestra in the 1920s, he became the sensation of the music halls, especially known for his expressive, melodic solos. [3] For Armstrong, improvisation was a tool with which the soloist could communicate his interpretation in the spur of the moment. [4] This individualistic approach to music has influenced countless successors. [5] He believed that improvisation should be a core feature of jazz and helped popularize its appeal.
8

8 ▬▬▬▬▬▬▬▬▬▬▬▬▬

To make this paragraph most logical, sentence 5 should be placed

A) where it is now.

B) after sentence 1.

C) after sentence 2.

D) after sentence 3.

The USA Patriot Act, signed into law by George W. Bush in the wake of 9/11 terrorist attacks, has become a contentious issue among Americans. The law allows the US government to monitor individuals that it considers dangerous through invasive means, such as phone records. Critics argue that the law violates citizens' right to privacy.

9 Proponents argue that the loss of privacy is warranted, given the immense benefit of preventing a national disaster. "Security comes before privacy," says one interviewee. "After all, if you have nothing to hide, why should it bother you?"

Since its launch in 1970, the Environment Protection Agency (EPA) has greatly contributed to the preservation of the nation's water, land, and air. [1] The EPA has led several cleanup initiatives to remedy the mistakes of the past. [2] In addition, it has worked tirelessly to demand that policymakers consider environmental costs. [3] Addressing the complex environmental issues facing the nation and the world requires cooperation among a diverse group of stakeholders. [4] Everyone has a role to play in creating a healthy, sustainable environment. [5] Although powerful, the EPA does not work alone. **10**

9

At this point, the writer is considering adding the following sentence.

Some welcome this expanded role the law grants the government, however.

Should the writer make this addition here?
A) Yes, because it provides a transition to the proponents' argument.
B) Yes, because it summarizes the main point of the previous paragraph.
C) No, because it is irrelevant to the discussion of privacy and technology.
D) No, because it blurs the focus of the paragraph by introducing an idea that goes unexplained.

10

To make this paragraph most logical, sentence 5 should be placed
A) where it is now.
B) after sentence 1.
C) after sentence 2.
D) after sentence 3.

According to the Korean Herald, chicken consumption per capita in South Korea has surpassed that of any other nation. The country's craze over *chimac*, a portmanteau for "chicken and beer," has created a cultural backdrop for the increased consumption. **11** A recent report suggests that the number of franchise-based fried chicken restaurants in Korea has surpassed the number of McDonald outlets worldwide.

11

At this point, the writer is considering adding the following sentence.

In addition, Korean fried chicken is poised to take on the world, as popular franchise brands like Kyochon and Pelicana gain recognition in America.

Should the writer make this addition here?

A) Yes, because it provides support for the paragraph's focus on the international appeal of Korean franchise restaurants.

B) Yes, because it provides a relevant detail about the popularity of Korean fried chicken.

C) No, because it undermines the main claim of the paragraph.

D) No, because it blurs the focus of the paragraph by introducing a loosely related detail.

On March, 1872, President Ulysses S. Grant signed the Act of Dedication, which created the Yellowstone National Park. Ferdinand Hayden, who explored the region under government sponsorship, was overjoyed as he believed in "setting aside the area as a pleasure ground for the benefit and enjoyment of the people." Some local residents, however, were disappointed and criticized the decision, expressing fear that the regional economy would not be able to thrive under the strict ban on mining, hunting and logging activities. **12**

12

At this point, the writer is considering adding the following sentence.

The residents' criticism stems from their adherence to the principles of Adam Smith's book, Wealth of Nations.

Should the writer make this addition here?

A) Yes, because it continues the explanation of the political views of the local residents.

B) Yes, because it reinforces the main point of the paragraph that the law was signed despite protest.

C) No, because it blurs the paragraph's main focus by introducing a new idea that is not clearly explained.

D) No, because it repeats information that has been provided earlier in the paragraph.

[1] Is there a biological distinction between the brain of a liberal and that of a conservative? [2] A recent study says yes. [3] A team of psychologists led by Professor Kanai of Sussex University, UK correlated the subjects' political leanings with their brain structures. [4] The study found that liberalism was associated with the gray matter volume of anterior cingulate cortex, while conservatism was associated with increased right amygdala size. [5] Although far from conclusive, the study suggests that certain cognitive styles of liberals and conservatives may be explained from a biological standpoint. [6] The anterior cingulate cortex is thought to be responsible for coping with complexities. [7] The amygdala is associated with anxiety and fear. **13**

13

To make this paragraph most logical, sentence 5 should be placed

A) where it is now.

B) after sentence 1.

C) after sentence 3.

D) after sentence 7.

[1] Automation of labor has been occurring all around us. [2] Simple jobs are being replaced by machines at an alarming rate. [3] Take, for example, the task of highway toll collection. [4] Nowadays, there are devices (such as EZpass) that automatically detect a moving vehicle and immediately deduct funds from the driver's bank account. [5] Some lament the loss of opportunity—being a toll collector was a comfortable government job offering a competitive salary and benefits. [6] Proponents of automation, however, argue that the era of manual labor for menial tasks is over and that humans should find more meaningful work that cannot be performed by machines. [7] With new and efficient technology, reliance on humans for toll collecting may be a relic of the past. **14**

14

To make the paragraph most logical, sentence 6 should be placed

A) where it is now.

B) after sentence 3.

C) after sentence 4.

D) after sentence 7.

[1] How can people become addicted to the Internet? [2] One possible explanation is that interfacing with digital content constitutes a reward center in the user's brain. [3] For example, online video games stimulate the same part of the brain as gambling does. [4] Even activities like surfing the web, using a dating site, browsing social media, and posting on a message board all involve seeking rewards of varying degrees. [5] Online contents offer unpredictable and variable reward structures, which elevate the mood of the user in ways other forms of addictive reward centers do. 15

15

To make this paragraph most logical, sentence 5 should be placed

A) where it is now.

B) after sentence 1.

C) after sentence 2.

D) after sentence 3.

[1] Policymakers in every country are faced with the significant challenge of meeting the healthcare needs of their populations, including those vulnerable communities in remote and rural areas. [2] In February 2009, following various international calls for action from global leaders, the World Health Organization (WHO) launched a program to increase access to health workers in remote and rural areas. [3] In order to ensure the equitable delivery of health services in these areas, skilled and motivated health workers need to be in the right place at the right time. [4] This program was developed in order to support countries to address the critical issues of retention and equitable distribution of health workers. [5] The program consists of three strategic pillars: building and sharing the evidence base, supporting countries in the analysis, and disseminating policy recommendations and guidelines. 16

16

To make this paragraph most logical, sentence 3 should be placed

A) before sentence 1

B) after sentence 1.

C) after sentence 2.

D) after sentence 4.

Launching an online shopping mall is no easy task. To start off, the entrepreneur must first purchase a desirable domain and secure it against any potential cyber criminals. To ensure a safe transaction space where no hacking could compromise the shoppers' personal information, it is paramount to invest in up-to-date security infrastructure. Unless the owner is an expert in such a field, it may be necessary to hire a professional. **17** Competition and turnover rates are also high, with 35% of all new businesses reportedly going under within the 2 years of launch.

17

The writer is considering deleting the sentence. Should the sentence be kept or deleted?

A) Kept, because it supports the main point of the paragraph that starting a new business is difficult.

B) Kept, because it provides a detail that supports the main topic of the paragraph.

C) Deleted, because it blurs the paragraph's focus with a loosely related detail.

D) Deleted, because it undermines the paragraph's claim that cybersecurity is important.

[1] A visit to the embassy requires jumping many hurdles, and I came prepared. [2] When I got to the embassy, I first provided my photo ID and proof of scheduled appointment. [3] The officer led me inside through the metal detector, and I was seated in the reception area with a numbered ticket in my hand. [4] The lady at the window could not be any more accommodating, though, and she looked through my documents with a pleasant smile. [5] The interview took only 5 minutes, at the conclusion of which I was stamped a permit for re-entry. **18**

18

The writer wants to add the following sentence to the paragraph.

The wait was arduous, and many who were sitting by me—by the looks on their faces—agreed with me.

The best placement for the sentence is immediately

A) after sentence 1.

B) after sentence 2.

C) after sentence 3.

D) after sentence 5.

Studying music can have a beneficial effect on the student. A 2013 report conducted by the University of Virginia found that students who study music showed higher aptitudes in pattern recognition and strategy development. These skills are invaluable for problem solving and can aid multiple career trajectories along the way. **19** That a fine art discipline can lead to success in other, lucrative fields can be a difficult concept to stomach, for sure.

19

The writer is considering adding the following sentence.

Mozart, for example, attributed his compositional success to his laser-fine focus on details.

Should the writer make this addition here?

A) Yes, because it provides a detail that supports the main topic of the paragraph.

B) Yes, because it reinforces the finding of the University of Virginia study that music develops higher aptitudes.

C) No, because it fails to support the paragraph's main claim that music helps develop skills that may be beneficial to other careers.

D) No, because it distracts from the focus of the paragraph.

In today's technologically advanced environment, there are many distractions **20** that can diminish a student's ability to focus on schoolwork. So, it is now more important than ever to exert strong self-control and allocate time wisely. Perhaps not surprisingly, there is an increasing demand for private study halls where all electronic devices are banned.

20

At this point, the writer is considering adding the following information.

—online VODs, mobile games, and text messenger applications—

Should the writer make this addition here?

A) Yes, because it provides relevant examples of distractions mentioned in the paragraph.

B) Yes, because it sets up argument in the paragraph that all electronic devices should be banned.

C) No, because it blurs the focus of the paragraph with a loosely related detail.

D) No, because it repeats information that has been provided earlier in the sentence.

[1] Technological innovation has transformed political activism. [2] Thanks to smartphones and the Internet, political movements can be quickly and effectively organized. [3] For example, the Arab Spring movement of 2011 utilized communication via Facebook and Twitter in order to mobilize thousands of protesters. [4] In addition to these platforms, new forms of digital activism are emerging. **21** [5] These movements seek to bring about change by putting political pressure on the existing infrastructure.

[1] Dr. Gardner of Harvard University developed the Multiple Intelligences Theory in 1983. [2] Claiming that the traditional standard of measuring intelligence, IQ, is inadequate, Gardner argued that there are 8 equally valuable types of intelligence. [3] Many schools have reevaluated their curricula to reflect Dr. Gardner's findings, yet much work remains to be done. [4] Plenty of schools still insist on rewarding only those who possess linguistic and logical intelligence. **22**

21

At this point, the writer is considering adding the following sentence.

The hacker group Anonymous has used "hacktivism," and whistleblowers like Edward Snowden have used "leaktivism" to call for change.

Should the writer make this addition here?

A) Yes, because it provides specific details about the kinds of digital activism that are emerging.

B) Yes, because it supports the main point of the paragraph that technology has transformed political activism.

C) No, because it provides a loosely related detail that interrupts the flow of the paragraph.

D) No, because it describes activities that are still considered illegal by many countries.

22

Where is the most logical place to add the following sentence?

Overall, his theory garnered positive response from the educators.

A) After sentence 1.

B) After sentence 2.

C) After sentence 3.

D) After sentence 4.

The recent article published by the New York Times entitled "The Blobs in your Tea? They're Supposed to Be There" was harshly criticized by the Los Angeles Times. [2] The critics point out that the Times reporter treated bubble tea—a staple dessert in Taiwan since the 1970s—as something "exotic and niche." [3] Other publications quickly followed suit. [4] Doing so, they allege, is a form of "Columbusing," or the act of claiming novelty or popularity when white people finally discover a long-existent phenomenon. **23**

23

To make this paragraph most logical, sentence 3 should be placed
A) where it is now.
B) before sentence 1.
C) after sentence 1.
D) after sentence 4.

Cicadas are a strange breed of insects that spend most of their life underground as larvae. Once a larva emerge out of the ground after anywhere between one to seventeen years (depending on species), it molts. **24** During the molting, the larva sheds its exoskeleton and emerge as the winged, sexually-reproductive adult. The adult cicada lives for about a week, during which it must find a mate and reproduce.

24

At this point, the writer is considering adding the following sentence.

Scientists warn that climate change may be changing the life cycle of cicadas; the affected insects are reportedly leaving the ground up to 4 years earlier than expected.

Should the writer make this addition here?
A) Yes, because it provides a transition from discussing the cicada's life cycle to a potential environmental problem.
B) Yes, because it provides a relevant statistic to support the main point of the paragraph.
C) No, because it fails to account for the differences in the species of cicadas and their life cycles.
D) No, because it interrupts the discussion of molting.

Critics have long held filmmaker Wes Anderson in high regard. **25** He is what many call an auteur—a singular artist who controls all aspects of a collaborative project. Known for his pastel—colored sets and soundtracks from the 1960s and 1970s, Anderson carefully curates every detail of his film in order to convey a sense of innocence and its loss in an unfeeling world. While many fledgling artists try their hands at such a holistic approach, it is difficult to pull off what Anderson does: without a clear, disciplined aesthetic, a film can easily feel "forced" or "inauthentic."

Although never formally declared a movement, the New Wave school had a profound impact on French filmmaking. The New Wave filmmakers were linked by their conscious rejection of the literary period pieces, their spirit of youthful experimentation, and their willingness to experiment with novel forms. In doing so, the New Wave sought to move beyond the parameters set by traditional filmmaking. For example, New Wave filmmakers engaged with the social and political upheavals of the **26** era.

25

The writer is considering deleting the underlined sentence. Should the writer make this change?

A) Yes, because it repeats information that has been provided earlier in the paragraph.

B) Yes, because it blurs the paragraph's focus by introducing a topic that is not further explained.

C) No, because it properly establishes the paragraph's focus on Anderson's approach to filmmaking.

D) No, because it explains why critics appreciate Anderson's work.

26

The writer is considering revising the underlined portion of the sentence to read:

era, making their radical experiments with editing, visual style, and narrative part of a general break with the conservative tradition.

Should the writer add this information here?

A) Yes, because it supports the paragraph's main claim that New Wave artists broke with tradition.

B) Yes, because it describes the political affiliations of the New Wave artists.

C) No, because it adds a loosely related detail about the artists' unhappiness with the conservative filmmaking.

D) No, because it undermines the main point of the paragraph that new styles are always better than the old.

[1] Cooking sprays are aerosol oil compounds that coat pots and pans without adding calories the way butter or other oils do. [2] Aside from oil, the sprays contain lecithin, an emulsifier, as well as nitrous oxide, carbon dioxide, or propane, which serve as a propellant. [3] Although representatives for top US brands like Pam and Crisco have declared their products perfectly safe for consumption, there has been an increase of pseudoscientific alarmist rhetoric against cooking sprays. [4] Needless to say, just because there are a few multisyllabic chemicals that the alarmists can't pronounce, it does not mean that cooking sprays are inherently harmful. [5] "Tell us the truth," the alarmists implore, asserting that the cooking spray's flammability somehow makes them a health hazard. **27**

27

To make the paragraph most logical, sentence 5 should be placed
A) where it is now.
B) after sentence 1.
C) after sentence 2.
D) after sentence 3.

[1] Can the artist be separated from the art? [2] How can we explain the bad—if not criminal— behavior of the artists that we hold so dear? [3] These perennial questions plague many fields of art, and jazz is no exception. [4] Less known, however, is the physical abuse that many of the jazzmen inflicted upon their spouses at home. [5] It is common knowledge that many of the greats of jazz have succumbed to substance abuse, whether it be alcohol or illicit drugs. [6] Miles Davis, the man behind every genre defining milestone in jazz, used to "beat his wife regularly," by his own admission. **28**

28

To make the paragraph most logical, sentence 4 should be placed
A) where it is now.
B) after sentence 1.
C) after sentence 5.
D) after sentence 6.

Lori Wesselhoff's new book, *Cat Gifs and Happiness*, seeks to analyze the public's online obsession over moving images (also known as gifs) of cats. The author argues that there is a primal force at work that orients the web surfer's attention to these cute felines in human situations. Take for example, the recent Internet hit involving cats grooming themselves as if they are taking a shower. **29** The looped images show a Persian Grey scrub itself in a manner eerily similar to the way a human might—soap bubbles and all. "It's an interspecies bonding," says Wesselhoff. "Humans are really seeing themselves in the cat, feeling a sense of solidarity despite the clear difference in biology."

29

At this point, the author is considering adding the following sentence.

In addition those of cats, there are gifs of all kinds of animals on the Internet, totalling up to a hundred-something zetabytes.

Should the writer make this addition here?

A) Yes, because it provides a transition from cat gifs to animal gifs discussed later in the paragraph.

B) Yes, because it reinforces the paragraph's main claim that there are many gifs online.

C) No, because it interrupts the flow of the paragraph's discussion of a recent phenomenon.

D) No, because it argues that humans are drawn to all kinds of images, not just those featuring cats.

Novelist Haruki Murakami's international popularity can be attributed to the following reasons. First, his recurring theme of isolation in an indifferent world is a welcome criticism of modernity. Second, the "magical realist" narratives bring fantastical elements that continually stimulate the readers' curiosity and keep heavy literary topics as engaging as light detective novels. **30** Finally, Murakami's novels feature strange, mysterious plots that the readers feel compelled to read on to find answers to.

30

The writer is considering deleting the underlined sentence. Should the sentence be kept or deleted?

A) Kept, because it provides a reason for Murakami's popularity.

B) Kept, because it reinforces the main point of the paragraph on the role of mystery in Murakami's work.

C) Deleted, because it provides a loosely related detail about Murakami's personal life.

D) Deleted, because it repeats information that has been provided earlier in the paragraph.

Genetically Modified Organisms (GMOs) have been on the receiving end of a vicious misinformation campaign. Whether genuinely concerned or irrationally lashing out, the opponents of GMO rely on shoddy evidence and propagate falsehoods. **31** A recent meta-study of over 6,000 peer reviewed studies of the past 20 years has revealed, once again, that GMOs are "perfectly safe for consumption," and that they even produce fewer mycotoxins than do non-GM crops.

31

The writer is considering adding the following sentence.

There is an overwhelming evidence that GMOs do not pose any threat.

Should the writer make this addition here?

A) Yes, because it provides a specific example of how the opponents of GMOs fail to cite relevant research.

B) Yes, because it provides a transition to the paragraph's next point about the safety of GMOs.

C) No, because it does not provide a detailed statistic in numbers.

D) No, because it inappropriately attacks the opponents of GMOs without letting them speak for themselves.

[1] While the subject matter is fascinating, there may not be too many career prospects for a dialectologist. [2] Melanie Cartier is a dialectologist who decided to leave the academia to pursue a career in film production. [3] She works as a dialect coach helping actors and actresses on the set. She has coached notable celebrities like Gwyneth Paltrow, Ewan McGregor, and Patrick Bateman. [4] "At first, the work was difficult to come by," says Cartier. [5] Most choose to be a scholar, dedicating their lives to research and, unfortunately, small pay. [6] "Having a linguistic sensitivity is paramount, but what really helped me get started was my networking skills." **32**

32

To make this paragraph most logical, this sentence 5 should be placed

A) after sentence 1.

B) after sentence 2.

C) after sentence 3.

D) after sentence 6.

Developing a disciplined practice routine is only the beginning of becoming a working musician, of course. Virtuosity at an instrument does not mean performance opportunities arise automatically. Not only do you need to have working relationships with other musicians but also you need to actively engage with performance venues, event promoters, and record company executives. **33** Cultivating a social media presence and developing a platform in which fans can interact either among them or with you may be even more important than playing well.

33

At this point, the writer is considering adding the following sentence.

Networking is an important skill a musician must possess.

Should the writer make this addition here?

A) Yes, because it provides support for the main point of the paragraph that it takes more than musical virtuosity to become a successful musician.

B) Yes, because it provides argument to forestall a potential objection to the main point.

C) No, because it repeats information that has been provided earlier in the paragraph.

D) No, because it blurs the focus of the paragraph by introducing a loosely related detail.

[1] Everyone's got an opinion, and that's been true forever and always. [2] However, never has the opinionated been given the gigantic mouthpiece in the form of online blogging so prevalent today. [3] Nowadays, any self-proclaimed expert can spread self-absorbed, meaningless opinions by sharing them online mercilessly, all while suffering a grandiose illusion that he or she is "contributing" to the world. [4] Blogging, unlike what these valiant tycoons of literary integrity may believe, is a difficult venture that takes dedication and talent to succeed. [5] In addition, he or she must not only be prolific but also profound and personable. [6] A successful blogger must be able to churn out content at regular intervals, with minimal interruptions. **34**

34

To make this paragraph most logical, sentence 6 should be placed

A) where it is now.

B) after sentence 2.

C) after sentence 3.

D) after sentence 4.

Until Pasteur, most people believed in "spontaneous generation." **35** According to this theory, living organisms could arise from inanimate matter, without descent from similar organisms. For example, people believed that mites arose from wood, maggots from rotting flesh, and tapeworms from blood. Pasteur was deeply suspicious of this theory and disproved it in his 1859 experiment involving boiled meat broth in a curved flask. In the experiment, Pasteur found out that microbes did not originate in the boiled broth itself but instead caused by a transmission from the air.

35

The writer is considering deleting the underlined sentence. Should the writer make this deletion?

A) Yes, because it repeats information that has been provided earlier in the paragraph.

B) Yes, because it blurs the focus of the paragraph by introducing an idea that goes unexplained.

C) No, because it provides an elaboration on a technical term that Pasteur later sought to disprove through his experiment.

D) No, because it introduces a logical conclusion to the paragraph.

[1] Chances are, if you have seen a marching band, you've probably seen a sousaphone. [2] It is a large brass instrument whose tubing goes all around the performer. [3] Like the tuba, the sound, which is first produced by buzzing the lips against a metal mouthpiece (or a cup), is amplified and projected through the tubing and out the bell. [4] The sousaphone was invented in 1893 by a man named J.W. Pepper, who, under the direction of John Philip Sousa, developed a version of tuba that is easier to hold while marching. [5] Aside from its maneuverability, the sousaphone features a slightly different method of projection. [6] However, unlike the tuba, which has a bell that points straight up, the later versions of the sousaphone had forward-facing bells. **36**

36

To make this paragraph most logical, sentence 3 should be placed

A) where it is now.

B) after sentence 1.

C) after sentence 5.

D) after sentence 6.

Are some people more likely than others to suffer skin damage from the sun? While everyone's skin can be affected by ultraviolet (UV) rays, people with light skin are much more likely to be damaged by the exposure. When the human skin is exposed to UV rays, it responds by releasing melanocytes, which regulate the production of melanin, **37** the pigment which darkens skin in the sun. When the skin darkens, it acts as a buffer against the release of cancer-causing free radicals. Because lighter skin lacks pathways for melanin production, it tends to burn instead of tan, a clear sign of skin damage.

The secret identity of the protagonist is a recurring theme in superhero stories. It is an effective storytelling tool that forges a sense of clandestine agreement between the narrative and the audience. The audience enters into a pact with Clark Kent, **38** a news reporter with a secret life as Superman, to keep his secret safe. Similar deals are struck with Peter Parker and Bruce Wayne—Spiderman and Batman, respectively. Therefore, the audience is provided an encompassing viewpoint from which the drama of the story unfolds.

37

The writer is considering deleting the underlined part of the sentence and ending the sentence with a period. Should the writer do this?

A) Yes, because it repeats information that has been provided earlier in the paragraph.

B) Yes, because it blurs the focus of the paragraph by introducing a loosely related detail.

C) No, because it reveals the author's true intentions for writing the paragraph.

D) No, because it provides a definition for a term that is central to the paragraph's main claim.

38

The writer is considering deleting the underlined part of the sentence. Should the writer make this deletion?

A) Yes, because it distracts from the paragraph's main point about Clark Kent.

B) Yes, because it interrupts the flow of the paragraph with a loosely related detail.

C) No, because it introduces the idea of a secret identity that will be repeated later in the paragraph.

D) No, because it provides a detail about the type of work that Clark Kent does.

The term "Mozart Effect" was coined by Alfred A. Tomatis, a music therapist who used Mozart's music to cure a variety of disorders. A follow-up study for Nature magazine suggested that listening to Mozart before an IQ exam temporarily boosted the test taker's score on one of the sections. **39** The Wechsler IQ test, for example, measures intelligence in verbal, working memory, perception, and processing speed. Catching on like wildfire, the Mozart Effect became a barely studied yet widely popular phenomenon. In fact, after learning about it, the Governor of Georgia mandated every newborn baby be provided with a classical music CD.

[1] The field of 3D printing promises a new technological age unhindered by the limitations of manufacturing, distribution, and retail. [2] From a bridge in Amsterdam to a wedding cake in New York City, 3D printing can do everything and more. [3] Futurists speculate that, as a whole, the technology can lay an important foundation to address the widespread poverty in the third world. [4] There are many countries in Asia and Africa, where modern infrastructure cannot take root easily, due to the prohibitive costs. [5] Even amputees from war-torn countries will be able to afford help in the form of 3D-printed prosthetics. **40**

39

The writer is considering deleting the sentence. Should the writer make this deletion?

A) Yes, because it interrupts the discussion of Mozart Effect with a loosely related detail about IQ testing.

B) Yes, because it undermines the paragraph's claim that all IQ tests have demonstrated positive effects of Mozart.

C) No, because it provides an example of an IQ test that could measure the significance of Mozart Effect.

D) No, because it provides an effective transition to the popularity of Mozart Effect by concluding the paragraph's point about IQ testing.

40

At this point, the writer is considering adding the following sentence.

3D printing hopes to lower the cost of production to mere fractions of the traditional methods so that even such countries can start building what they need.

To make this paragraph most logical, the sentenced should be placed

A) before sentence 1.

B) after sentence 1.

C) after sentence 3.

D) after sentence 4.

Chapter 2

Sentence Combination

Chapter Guide

Sentence Combination

1. Use the three-step-analysis. Evaluate answer choices based on

- Grammar
- Logic and Context
- Concision

First, check for **proper structure and punctuation.** Second, check if the sentence **keeps the intended meaning** and **uses proper transition words.** Finally, if any choices remain and they mean the same thing, **pick the more concise choice.**

The other lessons in this section apply this concept to isolated, more detailed cases.

2. SVO. O → SVO, which

By far the most common type of SC question features this format. If the object (or the last noun) in the first sentence is repeated as the subject of the second sentence, change the full independent clause into a relative pronoun clause (that, which, who, etc.).

3. Keep — Front modifiers, back modifiers.

Remember, the fewer S-V relationships you can have, the better. Modifier phrases and clauses are more likely to omit subjects and verbs and are therefore more concise.

4. Consider — Colons, em dashes

If there is a clear contextual clue that indicates restatement or elaboration, choices with colons and em dashes provide not only the correct logical relationship but also a concise structure.

5. Consider — Independent Clause (IC), Coordinating Conjunction (CC) + IC.

In structure questions, two independent clauses joined by a comma and a coordinating conjunction is a fantastic choice. In sentence combination questions, there is likely a better choice that results in more concise language. Since these choices are grammatically correct, keep them, but always check if the CC is used logically. Then check against other choices for concision.

6. Avoid — Being, Having, Means that, This is because.

These phrases tend to result in wordiness.

Example 1:

African-Americans were frustrated by the continued suppression of rights. They organized marches, lectures, and sit-ins, demanding reform of oppressive institutions.

Which choice best combines the underlined sentences?

A) Organizing marches, lectures, and sit-ins and demanding reform of oppressive institutions, African-Americans were frustrated by the continued suppression of rights.

B) Frustrated by the continued suppression of rights, African Americans organized marches, lectures, and sit-ins, demanding reform of oppressive institutions.

C) African-Americans were frustrated by the continued suppression of rights, which caused them to organize marches, lectures, and sit-ins in order to demand reform of oppressive institutions.

D) African-Americans who were frustrated by the continued suppression of rights and organized marches, lectures, and sit-ins eventually demanded reform of oppressive institutions.

The worst way to tackle a question like this is to go immediately to the choices. All choices will sound similar, and you will have to rely on your "ear" to tell them apart. Don't do that. Instead, try to group ideas in the sentence together first. The two ideas were that African-Americans were "frustrated" and that they consequently "organized." The correct choice will present this causal relationship in a logical, concise manner.

(A) reverses the relationship. Was frustration the result of organizing? Probably not.

(C) is wordy because of the phrase "which caused them."

(D) doesn't sound bad, but it does not give proper context to "organizing" as a result of "frustration."

(B) is the best choice. Note the use of the front modifier "frustrated," which avoids wordy things like pronouns and clauses.

Example 2:

    Rebellions broke out and were paused by the Peace of Augsburg in <u>1555. They officially established</u> northern Europe as a Protestant territory.

    Which choice best combines the sentences at the underlined portion?

A) 1555, which resulted in officially establishing

B) 1555, which officially established

C) 1555, and they officially established

D) 1555, which is what officially established

    Note that all choices are structurally sound and adequately punctuated. They pass on grammar. Note that all choices essentially say the same thing — that "establishing" happened. We must base our answer on concision here.

    (A) and (D) are easy to eliminate. "Resulted in establishing" and "which is what established" are wordy constructions that beat around the bush. Between the remaining choices, **(B)** should be preferred, because the relative pronoun clause "which established" is more concise than an independent clause "they established."

Chapter 2

Sentence Combination

Practice Questions

1 African-American music is often noted for its antiphonal structure. The lead performer makes a call, to which the rest of the ensemble responds.

1

Which choice most effectively combines the underlined sentences?

A) People often note African-American music for its antiphonal structure, which means that the lead performer makes a call and the rest of the ensemble responds.

B) African-American music is often noted for its antiphonal structure; moreover, the lead performer makes a call, to which the rest of the ensemble responds.

C) African-American music is well-known because of its antiphonal structure-the lead performer makes a call, to which the rest of the ensemble responds.

D) African-American music is often noted for its antiphonal structure, which features the lead performer making a call, to which the rest of the ensemble responds.

2 In the early 20th century, there was a group of like-minded composers. The group was known as the "Second Viennese School" and it changed Classical music forever.

2

Which choice most effectively combines the underlined sentences?

A) A group of composers known as the "Second Viennese School" arose in the early 20th century, and it changed Classical music forever.

B) Known as the "Second Viennese School," in the early 20th century, a group of like-minded composers changed Classical music forever.

C) In the early 20th century, a group of like-minded composers known as the "Second Viennese School" changed Classical music forever.

D) Classical music was changed forever in the 20th century, and a group called "the Second Viennese School" did so.

The proposed virtual reality headset would be able to pair up with a mobile device via bluetooth. **3** It would truly be an innovative gadget. A cutting-edge visual entertainment system would be available on-the-go.

3

Which choice most effectively combines the underlined sentences?

A) It would truly be an innovative gadget: a cutting-edge visual entertainment system would be available on-the-go.

B) A cutting-edge visual entertainment would be available on-the-go, and it would be an innovative gadget.

C) A cutting-edge visual entertainment system, an innovative gadget, would be available on-the-go.

D) With the gadget being truly innovative, a cutting-edge visual entertainment system would be available on-the-go.

In a notable exchange between Isaac Asimov and Kurt Vonnegut, the latter famously asked of the former, "How does it feel to know everything?" Asimov answered that he only had a feeling of **4** omniscience, and this instilled a feeling of unease.

4

Which choice most effectively combines the sentences at the underlined portion?

A) NO CHANGE

B) omniscience, which instilled

C) omniscience. This instilled

D) omniscience,

5 Writers often resort to certain rituals in order to focus their attention to the task at hand. Many painters report they travel, especially to naturally scenic spots, to meditate on their subject.

5

Which choice most effectively combines the underlined sentences?

A) To focus their attention to the task at hand, writers often resort to certain rituals, which is similar to how many painters travel to naturally scenic spots to meditate on their subjects.

B) Many painters report they travel to naturally scenic spots to meditate on their subject, while writers often resort to certain rituals in order to focus their attention to the task at hand.

C) Many painters are similar to writers in deciding to travel to scenic spots to meditate on their subject, just like how the writers resort to certain rituals in order to focus their attention.

D) Just as writers often resort to certain rituals in order to focus, painters travel to naturally scenic spots to meditate.

In an infamous battle over creative license, Milli Vanilli accused Vanilla Ice of stealing the former's **6** music, Vanilla Ice did this by plagiarizing the bass riff from *Girl You Know It's True*.

6

A) music by plagiarizing

B) music, which is what Vanilla Ice tried to do when he plagiarized

C) music, and Vanilla Ice plagiarized

D) music, by which Vanilla Ice plagiarized

Gun advocates believe that any effort to ban firearms violates citizens' Second Amendment right. The proponents for gun control, however, believe the **7** opposite. They argue that banning assault rifles and high capacity magazines would preserve the forefathers' intended vision of firearm ownership, all while allowing hobbyists to keep guns for hunt and protection.

7

Which choice most effectively combines the sentences at the underlined portion?

A) opposite, which is

B) opposite; their argument is

C) opposite—

D) opposite, such

Cicadas usually appear out of the ground by late-June or **8** early-July. This follows the long nymph stage of thirteen years.

8

Which choice most effectively combines the sentences at the underlined portion?

A) early-July, and this appearance follows

B) early-July, and the appearing follows

C) early-July and at the end of

D) early-July, following

Researchers have found that children who were exposed to music education fared better than other students in tasks involving abstract thinking and **9** logic. These findings are substantiated by standardized test scores.

9

Which choice most effectively combines the sentences at the underlined portion?

A) logic, according to the substantiation

B) logic, because the findings are substantiated

C) logic, as substantiated

D) logic, being substantiated

10 Actually, personal fitness coaches are trained in wide-ranging physical disciplines. They are martial arts, track, and weightlifting.

10

Which choice most effectively combines the underlined sentences?

A) Actually, personal fitness coaches are trained in wide-ranging physical disciplines, many of which include martial arts, track, and weightlifting.

B) Actually, personal fitness coaches, trained in martial arts, track, and weightlifting, have wide-ranging physical backgrounds.

C) Actually, personal fitness coaches are trained in wide-ranging physical disciplines, which include martial arts, track, and weightlifting.

D) Actually, wide-ranging physical disciplines are trained by personal fitness coaches, who study martial arts, track, and weightlifting.

The throne room of the fallen empire was rather modestly **11** adorned. Its ornamental drapes, carpets, and jewels retained the luster of regal dignity.

11

Which choice most effectively combines the sentences at the underlined portion?

A) adorned by its

B) adorned: its

C) adorned, while

D) adorned, but its

It is not at all clear at what age we should introduce smartphones to our young. **12** Smartphones rob children's attention aside from harming eyesight. They are likely to take up at least 25 to 50 percent of a child's free time.

12

Which choice most effectively combines the underlined sentences?

A) Robbing children's attention, aside from being harmful to eyesight, and the fact they are likely to take up at least 25 to 50 percent of a child's free time are what make smartphones dangerous.

B) Aside from harming eyesight, smartphones rob children's attention, likely taking up at least 25 to 50 percent of a child's free time.

C) Likely taking up at least 25 to 50 percent of a child's free time, smartphones rob children's attention and are harmful to eyesight.

D) Smartphones, which rob children's attention and harm their eyesight, are likely to take up at least 25 to 50 percent of a child's free time.

Cryosurgery, or the use of low temperatures to a specific site of lesion, has received positive feedback from surgeons who administered the technique as part of cancer treatment. **13** Cold liquid nitrogen isolates the diseased cells when applied to lesions. This isolation allows the surgeon to safely remove the cancerous area, without harming other parts of the body.

13

Which choice most effectively combines the underlined sentences?

A) When applied to lesions, cold liquid nitrogen isolates the diseased cells, allowing the surgeon to safely remove the cancerous area, without harming other parts of the body.

B) The surgeon is allowed to remove the cancerous area without harming other parts of the body because cold liquid nitrogen isolates the diseased cells when applied to lesions.

C) Cold liquid nitrogen isolates the diseased cells, when applied to lesions, the surgeon is allowed to remove the cancerous cells without harming the other areas of the body,

D) Without harming other parts of the body, the surgeon is allowed to remove the cancerous cells, because cold liquid nitrogen isolates the diseased cells when applied to lesions.

The news of James W. Marshall's discovery of gold in 1848 sparked a nation hungry for exploration and wealth. **14** The result was the California Gold Rush of 1849, a massive settlement of adventurers looking to hit paydirt.

14

A) NO CHANGE

B) The result was a massive settlement—the California Gold Rush of 1849—of adventurers looking to hit paydirt.

C) The result was adventurers looking to hit paydirt, a massive settlement known as the California Gold Rush of 1849.

D) The California Gold Rush of 1849 resulted and it was a massive settlement of adventurers looking to hit paydirt.

For added security, the entrance is monitored by a closed-circuit camera and an alarm **15** system. Such equipments guarantee an immediate response in the case of unauthorized intrusion.

15

Which choice most effectively combines the sentences at the underlined portion?

A) system, which guarantee

B) system and guarantees

C) system, and these equipments guarantee

D) system, since they guarantee

For Richard Nixon, promising the U.S. exit of Vietnam was a brilliant campaigning tool that could bring together the nation divided on the issue of antiwar **16** protest. He didn't have to side with the protesters or the anti-protesters.

16

Which choice most effectively combines the sentences at the underlined portion?

A) protest while still not having to

B) protest; however, he didn't have to

C) protest without having

D) protest, and he wasn't having

On this Black Friday, stores nationwide will be inundated by some 115 million **17** shoppers. They spend $850 on average in preparation for the holiday season.

17

Which choice most effectively combines the sentences at the underlined portion?

A) shoppers, with

B) shoppers, who spend

C) shoppers; and they are

D) shoppers, yet they will spend

With the advent of electronic filing of documents, some lawyers let go of any traditional filing **18** clerks. Other lawyers assign such staff members to other duties, like managing the office or assisting the paralegals.

18

Which choice most effectively combines the sentences at the underlined portion?

A) clerks, and other lawyers assign

B) clerks; meanwhile, other lawyers assign

C) clerks, while others assign

D) clerks: assigning

SHU, or Scoville Hotness Unit, is a standard of measurement for capsaisinoid concentration in peppers. Bhut jolokia, commonly known as "ghost pepper," boasts its pungency at over 1 million [19] SHU. This is much hotter than the SHU of the beloved jalapeno, a common pepper often pickled to reduce its biting heat.

19

Which choice most effectively combines the sentences at the underlined portion?

A) SHU, which is

B) SHU; therefore, this is

C) SHU —

D) SHU, which means that it is

People who are well adjusted try to look on the bright side in the face of negative stimuli. [20] Those who are depressive, though, tend to dwell in and enumerate their miseries. They act that way, often day in and day out, until life becomes an , unfathomable darkness.

20

Which choice most effectively combines the underlined sentences?

A) Those who are depressive, though, tend to dwell in and enumerate their miseries, which they do day in and day out until life becomes an unfathomable darkness.

B) Those who are depressive, though, tend to, often day in and day out, dwell in and enumerate their miseries, which means life becomes an unfathomable darkness.

C) Although many who are depressive, though, tend to dwell in and enumerate their miseries, they do so, day in and day out, until life becomes an unfathomable darkness.

D) Those who are depressive, though, tend to dwell in and enumerate their miseries, day in and day out, until life becomes an unfathomable darkness.

Jazz guitarists traditionally prefer thicker strings with higher gauges. **21** Playing the guitar becomes somewhat difficult. The resulting timbre is apparently thicker and smoother.

22 Korea gained momentum in its quest to become the tech giant of the twenty-first century. It was propelled by the unparalleled success in the IT sector.

21

Which choice most effectively combines the underlined sentences?

A) Although playing the guitar becomes somewhat difficult, the resulting timbre is apparently thicker and smoother.

B) The resulting timbre is apparently thicker and smoother, however; playing the guitar becomes somewhat difficult.

C) The resulting timbre is apparently thicker and smoother; instead, playing the guitar becomes somewhat difficult.

D) Playing the guitar becomes somewhat difficult, because the resulting timbre is apparently thicker and smoother.

22

Which choice most effectively combines the underlined sentences?

A) Korea was propelled by the unparalleled success in the IT sector; it gained momentum in its quest to become the tech giant of the twenty-first century.

B) Korea, gaining momentum in its quest to become the tech giant of the twenty-first century, was propelled by the unparalleled success in the IT sector.

C) Propelled by the unparalleled success in the IT sector, Korea gained momentum in its quest to become the tech giant of the twenty-first century.

D) Gaining momentum in its quest to become the tech giant of the twenty-first century was what allowed Korea to be propelled by the unparalleled success in the IT sector.

Carl Jung posited that beneath the observable human psyche lay the "shadow," a repressed, dark personality.
23 His disciples were deeply influenced by the theory. Then, they applied this concept to analyze human societies.

23

Which choice most effectively combines the underlined sentences?

A) His disciples were deeply influenced by the theory; after that, they applied this concept to analyze human societies.

B) His disciples applied this concept to analyze human societies because they were influenced by the theory.

C) His disciples were deeply influenced by the theory, which they applied in order to analyze human societies.

D) Deeply influenced by the theory, his disciples applied this concept to analyze human societies.

Within two weeks, valuables ranging from jewelries to laptops have disappeared. **24** The items reported missing were all from the cafeteria building. In response, the University issued a campus-wide larceny warning.

24

Which choice most effectively combines the sentences at the underlined portion?

A) disappeared, and the items reported missing were all

B) disappeared—all

C) disappeared, all of which were

D) disappeared—all missing and all from

In commitment to using green energy, the company installed the state-of-art solar panels. 25 These not only greatly reduced the energy cost but also updated the appearance of the company building.

25

Which choice most effectively combines the sentences at the underlined portion?

A) panels, which

B) panels in order to

C) panels, the reason for their installation is

D) panels; with them the company

Much of St. Augustine's philosophy can be traced to his seminal work, _Confessions._ **26** The book outlines his sinful youth leading up to his conversion to Christianity.

26

Which choice most effectively combines the sentences at the underlined portion?

A) _Confessions_, and the book

B) _Confessions_, in which he

C) _Confessions_; hence, the book

D) _Confessions_, which

The primitive form of electronic message transmission can be traced up to the telegraph. Even instant messaging—then referred to as IM—was commonplace in the **27** 90s. The actual term, "texting," sees prevalent use after the new millennium, along with the advent of social networking sites and smartphones.

27

Which choice most effectively combines the sentences at the underlined portion?

A) 90s; also the

B) 90s, and the

C) 90s, but the

D) 90s; whereas the

Sometimes, language can exhibit different levels of sophistication based on the culture's familiarity of the subject.
For example, the common name for _Seriola lalandi_ in English is always **28** yellowtail. The Japanese nomenclature varies based on the size of the fish—from _buri_ to _hamachi_.

28

Which choice most effectively combines the sentences at the underlined portion?

A) yellowtail, even though the

B) yellowtail; hence, the

C) yellowtail, whereas

D) yellowtail; likewise

Igor Stravinsky's early career is indebted to his Russian mentor, Rimsky-Korsakov.
Emerging toward the end of his "Russian period" was the orchestral work **29** _The Rite of Spring._ The piece was a meditation of paganistic raw energy.

29

Which choice most effectively combines the sentences at the underlined portion?

A) _The Rite of Spring_ and

B) _The Rite of Spring_; the piece was

C) _The Rite of Spring_, yet the piece was

D) _The Rite of Spring_,

The theory of wave-particle duality holds that every particle is also a wave — and vice versa. **30** As predicted by the theory, the elementary particles' wave-like character has been verified. By the same principle, atoms' wave-like character has been verified as well.

30

Which choice most effectively combines the underlined sentences?

A) As predicted by the theory, not only elementary particles but also atoms possess wave-like character, and they have been verified as well.

B) The elementary particles' wave-like character, in addition to that of the atoms, has been predicted and verified as well.

C) As predicted by the theory, the elementary particles' wave-like character has been verified, although atoms' wave-like character has been verified as well.

D) As predicted by the theory, the wave-like characters of both elementary particles and atoms have been verified.

Though often described as a loose collective of ragtag social dissidents, Occupy Wall Street brought together activists from wide ranging perspectives under a common **31** goal; it was to unite against the capitalist machinery and dismantle the perpetuation of economic inequality.

31

A) goal, which was

B) goal; its purpose was

C) goal, for it was

D) goal —

32 Ronald Reagan was known for his charming good looks, down-to-earth approachability, and pragmatic pro-business messages. Due to these qualities of his, he was able to emerge victorious in the presidential election of 1980.

32

Which choice most effectively combines the sentences at the underlined portion?

A) Ronald Reagan was known for his charming good looks, down-to-earth approachability, and pragmatic pro-business messages, and because of them, he

B) Because Ronald Reagan was known for his charming good looks, down-to-earth approachability, and pragmatic pro-business messages, he

C) Known for his charming good looks, down-to-earth approachability, and pragmatic pro-business messages, Ronald Reagan

D) Ronald Reagan knew he had advantages such as his charming good looks, down-to-earth approachability, and pragmatic pro-business messages; consequently, he

Neoliberal globalism, as envisioned by the President Clinton and further propagated by President Obama, suffered a harsh voter referendum and **33** backlash. It was evidenced by the victory of Donald Trump, who ran on the platform of anti-interventionism.

33

Which choice most effectively combines the sentences at the underlined portion?

A) backlash; therefore, it was

B) backlash,

C) backlash, although

D) backlash, and this was

3D printing has allowed for easy, cost-effective production of **34** prosthetics; thanks to the new technology. More amputees are likely to receive treatments they not only can afford but also deserve.

34

Which choice most effectively combines the sentences at the underlined portion?

A) NO CHANGE

B) prosthetics, thanks to the new technology. More

C) prosthetics, thanks to the new technology, more

D) prosthetics. Thanks to the new technology, more

In his new book, Richard Dawkins offers a biting criticism on **35** theism. In it he offers an atheist's defense against the charges of amorality.

35

Which choice most effectively combines the sentences at the underlined portion?

A) theism, in which

B) theism and

C) theism —

D) theism, which is

During the Enlightenment, French intellectuals met in each other's living rooms—known as salons—to discuss the matters of art, politics, and philosophy. Writers, musicians, and activists, as well as anyone with an open **36** mind, gathered. They did so clandestinely, as to be secluded from the public's intrusion.

36

Which choice most effectively combines the sentences at the underlined portion?

A) mind, gathered; they did it

B) mind, gathered

C) mind gathered

D) mind, gathered —

Facebook has been a leader in defining the role of social media in a world increasingly absent of boundaries. **37** Mark Zuckerberg is the founder and CEO. He believes that social networking sites bring a unique method of communication that seeks not only to share data but also human emotions.

37

Which choice most effectively combines the sentences at the underlined portion?

A) Mark Zuckerberg, the founder and CEO, believes

B) Mark Zuckerberg, whose role is the founder and CEO, believes

C) The belief of Mark Zuckerberg, the founder and CEO, is

D) Mark Zuckerberg is the founder and CEO who believes

Franz Kafka's works deal with an individual's sense of loss in a world filled with matter-of-fact, bureaucratic indifference. Kafka's astute observation was widely influential in literary **38** circles. It led to the coining of a new adjective, *kafkaesque*, to refer to the sense of loss.

38

Which choice most effectively combines the sentences at the underlined portion?

A) circles, and it was leading

B) circles; leading

C) circles, leading

D) circles leading

Continued acts of rebellion swept the colonies, as Americans were incensed by the tyrannical British tax codes. Colonists organized a mass dumping of British **39** tea. The dumping took place in Boston, MA. Samuel Adams defended the act as a principled protest and the only option for people to demonstrate their rights.

39

Which choice most effectively combines the sentences at the underlined portion?

A) NO CHANGE.

B) tea, taking place in Boston, MA and defending

C) tea in Boston, MA, which Samuel Adams defended

D) tea, which Samuel Adams defended in Boston, MA

Some of the Solar System's moons, such as Neptune's Triton and Saturn's Phoebe, are said to have originated from **40** somewhere far away. They are likely to have originated from a location known as the Kuiper Belt.

40

Which choice most effectively combines the sentences at the underlined portion?

A) somewhere far away

B) somewhere far away, which is

C) somewhere:

D) somewhere; it is a location

Chapter 3

Transition Words

Chapter Guide

System of Equalities/Inequalities

First things first: transition word questions test you on your ability to **utilize context clues to infer logical relationship** between sentences or paragraphs. Consider the following example:

In the 1990s, the American Heart Association (AHA) launched a massive awareness campaign alerting the public to the dangers of fat-heavy diets. Today, <u>for example,</u> reflecting the shift in dietary habits, the organization voices warning against carbohydrates.

1. Do not read the transition word.
   - Your brain is wired to see connections in disparate ideas. By reading the transition words, you are likely to consider what's written as logically sound.
2. Make a prediction before evaluating choices.
   - As always, being able to predict will **save time** and **increase accuracy.**
3. Eliminate any synonymous choices.
   - Imagine "for example" and "for instance" are offered in the same question. In this case, you can safely assume neither one can be correct, because they are interchangeable.

Now, let's evaluate the choices.

(A) NO CHANGE
(B) in fact,
(C) as a result,
(D) however,

SAT will give you contextual clues to help you. In this example, phrases "in the 1990s" and "today" tell you that we are dealing with two different time periods. "Fat-heavy diets" and "carbohydrates" stand against each other, as well. If you are able to identify these opposites, it becomes clear we're looking for a transition of **contrast.** The correct choice is **(D).**

Note that "however" is by far the most common answer in transition word questions; however, frequency is never the best guidepost. Learn the following common transition words and their relatives.

Common Transition Words

	Function	Similar Words
However	Show contrast in idea or betrayal of expectation.	nonetheless, nevertheless, on the other hand, alternatively, in contrast, conversely, at the same time, still, instead, while, despite, even though, although, but, yet
Similarly	Set up comparison	likewise, in the same way, in the same manner
For example	Provide example	for instance, specifically, namely, in other words
Consequently	Show cause and effect	therefore, thus, hence, as a result, because, due to, accordingly
Furthermore	Provide additional information	in addition, to add, additionally, moreover, besides
In fact	Provide emphasis	indeed, above all
To this end	Demonstrate purpose	in order to, for this purpose

**Note that functions of certain expressions are more than one. Take "in fact," for example. It could serve as an emphasis if affirming the previous idea, and it could serve as a contrast if introducing a contradictory idea.

**Note that while many of the transition words are conjunctive adverbs, they do not have to be. Coordinating conjunctions (FANBOYS) and subordinating conjunctions (although, while, because, etc.) also describe logical relationships. Consider appropriate grammatical constructions for these cases. For example:

Due to their stripes, Okapis are reminiscent of zebras, <u>however,</u> they are actually more closely related to giraffes.

A) NO CHANGE

B) but,

C) nevertheless,

D) although,

There is a betrayal of expectation here, so "however" seems like an appropriate choice. Because conjunctive adverbs cannot join two independent clauses together, however, the sentence is grammatically incorrect. Eliminate (A) and (C), for the same error. Using "although" seems plausible, but the comma disqualifies it. The answer is **(B).**

Chapter 3

Transition Words

Practice Questions

Because new apps like Uber and Lyft connect passengers to drivers automatically, the way people use taxis has been revolutionized. **1** By contrast, tech-savvy young city dwellers can now schedule their travels at a negotiable price point.

1

A) NO CHANGE
B) Besides,
C) For example,
D) Nonetheless,

"Tell not the enemy that I am slain, for the battle rages on." Admiral Yi Soon Shin left these last words as he perished in a battle during the Japanese Invasion of 1594. With his last breath, he bolstered his soldiers' morale. **2** Furthermore, inspired by their fallen leader's noble words, the soldiers fought courageously to fend off the Japanese.

2

A) NO CHANGE
B) As a result,
C) Nevertheless,
D) DELETE the underlined portion and begin the sentence with a capital letter.

Online postings to fill full-time positions can be inundated with applications, especially if corporate jobs are offered. A handwritten "Help Needed" notice displayed on a window of a small bakery, **3** therefore, may go unnoticed for months before garnering a response.

3

A) NO CHANGE
B) however,
C) in effect,
D) as a rule,

There is growing criticism that advancement of technology widens the gap of wealth between classes. Those with means, who could afford the latest innovations, tend to come out ahead. Technology that could be used to better the society, in turn, ends up as a means of oppression by the wealthy few. **4** In addition, certain technologies could actively eliminate employment opportunities traditionally afforded to the lower classes.

4

A) NO CHANGE
B) However,
C) Thus,
D) Conversely,

YouTube, as a visual media outlet, allowed online activism to be both personal and accessible. One prominent videographer boasting 800,000 subscribers, **5** in any case, specializes in presenting quirky social issues that go largely unnoticed by traditional network news channels.

5

A) NO CHANGE
B) therefore,
C) for example,
D) however,

A new study from 2016 revealed that laws requiring voters to present IDs at voting sites disproportionately affect minority voters, who are less likely to possess government ID. The research found that "strict photo identification laws have a clear negative impact on the turnout of Hispanics, Blacks, and mixed-race Americans in primaries and general elections." **6** For example, the authors of the study called for repeals of such state laws, which had been prevalent in the South and the Midwest.

6

A) NO CHANGE
B) Subsequently,
C) However,
D) Similarly,

Since the Industrial Revolution, the right to a fair wage has been a contentious issue between business owners and workers. Due to the imbalance of power, there has been pushback at every turn against raising wages. **7** Therefore, if not been for the labor unions' persistent strikes, forcing the capitalists to the negotiation table, today's minimum wage would be much lower.

7

A) NO CHANGE
B) Indeed,
C) Nevertheless,
D) However,

According to Dunning and Kruger's landmark study, those who are incompetent are more likely to overestimate their aptitude. **8** In addition, those who are actually well qualified for a task are likely to underestimate their aptitude.

8

A) NO CHANGE
B) Thus,
C) Despite this,
D) On the other hand,

The Fourth Industrial Revolution, characterized by the combination of physical, digital, and biological forces, may have arrived. According to futurists like Ray Kurzweil, this development will significantly alter the human experience, because the rate of technological advancement will rapidly accelerate. They argue that the Fourth Industrial Revolution, **9** nevertheless, is the most radical change that human societies have ever experienced.

9

A) NO CHANGE

B) however,

C) yet,

D) then,

With sea levels on the rise, nature has issued its warning to us. **10** Therefore, we should continue to support the environmental movement not just because it is the right thing to do, but also because it is necessary for our survival.

10

A) NO CHANGE

B) However,

C) For example,

D) Instead

Eating local and sustainable foods does not only benefit the consumers but also the producers. **11** Regardless, both consumers and producers should consider themselves allies and partners in supporting a just cause.

11

A) NO CHANGE

B) Nevertheless,

C) Similarly,

D) Accordingly,

Yelp reviews left by approximately 1,000 users range from one to five stars, with the highest and the lowest ratings appearing in the highest frequencies. **12** Besides that, this statistic articulates a common theme across many other online platforms—people of extreme opinions are more likely to express their thoughts.

12

A) NO CHANGE

B) Around the same time,

C) Nevertheless,

D) DELETE the underlined portion and begin the sentence with a capital letter.

When a computer game cafe opened in its neighborhood, the university was torn by controversy. Most students, as expected, were overjoyed; **13** for example, others who viewed gaming as a bad habit and a danger to youth worried that the cafe would lure students away from their primary concern at university—study.

13

A) NO CHANGE
B) however,
C) specifically,
D) in fact,

Wynton Marsalis' interpretation of jazz as a continuation of the New Orleans tradition is decidedly neoclassical. He argues that swing rhythm and blues sensibilities are essential to the genre and must be preserved. **14** In short, neoclassicists like Marsalis include these traditional elements and reinterpret them in innovative ways.

14

A) NO CHANGE
B) By the same token,
C) To this end,
D) Nonetheless,

Although Enrico Fermi's famous paradox has enjoyed much attention since its introduction in the 1950s, it was severely criticized in a 1985 paper by Robert Freitas. **15** At this time, Freitas argued that Fermi relied to heavily on propositional logic and that using modal logic would prove the paradox mistaken.

15

A) NO CHANGE
B) In the paper,
C) On one hand,
D) Next,

Ever since electronics—such as phones and music players—became portable, American schools have had to adopt stringent "No Gadget" policies. **16** Still, teachers may confiscate cell phones, mp3 players, and digital cameras until the end of a school day.

16

A) NO CHANGE
B) Furthermore,
C) For example,
D) However,

A popular mode of instruction, the Socratic method nonetheless has its share of detractors. Critics argue that it actually hinders the students learning process. Because Socratic method puts a spotlight on a chosen student, it puts intense pressure on the individual. In addition, because it involves the instructor and the student in an isolated event, the classroom becomes a spectacle, with active participants and spectators. **17** Consequently, the Socratic method may be a preferred mode of instruction for some teachers, but it does have downsides.

17

A) NO CHANGE
B) Despite this,
C) In other words,
D) Therefore,

Income is clearly an indicator of happiness. Take, for example, the humanity's situation before the 19th century. Child mortality was over 50 percent, food was scarce, and most of one's life was spent producing food. The increased average income of the modern society has removed these ills. **18** However, the increased income—and the resulting relative comfort—does not necessarily mean that people are happier today than they were in 1700.

18

A) NO CHANGE
B) Moreover,
C) Subsequently,
D) Accordingly

Orthodontists have universally adopted new invisible plastic braces for tooth correction. Compared to their steel cousins, plastic braces are more cosmetically appealing and hygienic. **19** Also, the new braces only need to be worn for six to eighteen months, which means they are cost-effective.

19

A) NO CHANGE
B) In other words,
C) Therefore,
D) For instance,

Typically, northern landbirds such as swallows make long flights to the tropics during winter. **20** For example, during an especially cold winter of 2015, such landbirds were recorded migrating as early as September.

20

A) NO CHANGE

B) As such,

C) Moreover,

D) However,

The dormitory is equipped with a study lounge, complete with desks, chairs, and lamps. **21** However, the study lounge walls are made soundproof as to help students concentrate during stressful exam seasons.

21

A) NO CHANGE

B) Likewise,

C) In addition to these,

D) For these reasons,

Though many mock cryptozoology—the study of secret animals—as a useless discipline fantasizing about myths like Bigfoot or the Loch Ness Monster, it has actually contributed to modern understanding of the animal kingdom. **22** In contrast, gorillas were once considered to be mythical ape men similar to Bigfoot, until they were discovered during a 1902 expedition led by a group of cryptozoologists.

22

A) NO CHANGE

B) In broad terms,

C) For example,

D) Nevertheless,

A recent poll by Gallup showed that only twenty percent of the voters approved of Congress' performance. **23** Therefore, the President's approval rating sank to an all time low—at thirty-five percent.

23

A) NO CHANGE

B) Moreover,

C) However,

D) Thus,

An increase in the price of ingredients forced the restaurant to announce a considerable hike on the prices of its menu offerings. **24** Consequently, some long time customers complained and declared they would take their business elsewhere.

24

A) NO CHANGE

B) However,

C) Nevertheless,

D) Previously,

When I visited Los Angeles for the first time, I fully expected to bask in the sun and enjoy outdoor activities. **25** On one hand, I couldn't wait to go watch the passersby at Venice Beach. Much to my dismay, however, the weather was atrocious for the entirety of my visit.

25

A) NO CHANGE

B) Similarly,

C) However,

D) For instance,

Introducing natural predators to control pests is an ancient practice that dates back to 300 AD. During China's Jin Dynasty, Ji Han, a botanist, described a process in which a large species of ant is introduced to a field of citrus fruit trees infested with a smaller species of ant. The larger ants scare off the others, allowing the trees to grow undisturbed. Without the larger ants, **26** consequently, the trees may become barren, completely unable to yield fruit.

26

A) NO CHANGE

B) hence,

C) however,

D) likewise,

Cold brew coffee has entered the scene in full-force, establishing yet another trend among coffee lovers worldwide. The brewing technique, which takes 12 hours per batch, is said to yield flavors that are smooth and lush, with a distinct mildness. Some coffee critics, however, believe that this lack of bitterness is actually a major flaw. They allege, **27** likewise, that long exposure to air produces a flat taste devoid of any complexity.

27

A) NO CHANGE

B) in addition,

C) conversely,

D) therefore,

Bioluminescence, the production of light by a living organism, has many different functions in nature. Some species depend on body-generated light to attract mates or prey. Others, **28** alternatively, use their light to warn or scare off predators.

28

A) NO CHANGE
B) finally,
C) on the other hand,
D) despite this,

In his early years, Salvador Dali championed anarchism and communism, often making radical statements stemming from these political ideologies. **29** Also, such statements were crafted to inspire shock: they demonstrated the artist's showmanship, rather than his true convictions.

29

A) NO CHANGE
B) However,
C) Although,
D) Moreover,

Although internet router companies like Netgear and Linksys advertise the lightning fast speeds of their products, the jury is still out on whether a router's speed actually matters for the average user. A recent consumer report has identified, **30** however, that the router's speed is hard-capped by the bandwidth provided by an ISP and therefore cannot guarantee the advertised speed.

30

A) NO CHANGE
B) subsequently,
C) furthermore,
D) in fact,

Although opponents of genetically modified organisms (GMOs) argue that altered vegetables and meats are hazardous for consumption, such a claim has not been verified by scientific research. **31** In addition, in the most comprehensive GMO study conducted by the University of California Davis Department of Animal Science, genetically engineered animals were shown to be perfectly safe to eat.

31

A) NO CHANGE
B) However,
C) For instance,
D) Conversely,

The popularity of star chefs like the notorious Gordon Ramsay gives the impression that the chef is an emperor reigning over his kitchen and servants, who must be ready to yield to any edict. In reality, a chef must juggle numerous responsibilities, which include managing a kitchen full of skilled workers, communicating with the front-of-the-house, and making sure patrons are happy. **32** Therefore, those who dream of becoming a chef should possess strong communication skills.

32

A) NO CHANGE

B) However,

C) Nevertheless,

D) Initially,

Since its inception in the 1990s and unhindered growth throughout the 2000s, K-Pop has achieved ubiquitous cultural status in Korea and beyond. **33** However, the music is so popular in Seoul that you cannot walk a block or watch a minute of television without encountering the catchy beats and the elaborate choreography.

33

A) NO CHANGE

B) Even so,

C) According to its history,

D) In fact,

Contemporary psychology has largely discredited many of Sigmund Freud's assertions regarding the layered construction of the self. The Austrian psychologist's influence remains, **34** however, in the practice of modern psychotherapy, where the counselor and the patient engage in one-on-one conversations for diagnosis.

34

A) NO CHANGE

B) therefore,

C) likewise,

D) conversely,

For bohemian types, life in the city has grown quite difficult. As recently as the 1980s, artists in Brooklyn could live in a small studio furnished with simple bedding and a kitchen for under 400 dollars a month. The same apartment in today's market, **35** subsequently, costs upwards of 800 dollars a month.

35

A) NO CHANGE

B) in contrast,

C) as a result,

D) consequently,

Traditionally, the role of the First Lady is to promote a general well-being of the population at large, tackling issues that are less prone to sharp political divides. Michelle Obama was no exception. **36** <u>Therefore</u>, she is credited with initiating the Let's Move Initiative, aimed at reducing childhood obesity by promoting a healthy diet and an active lifestyle.

36

A) NO CHANGE

B) For instance,

C) Indeed,

D) In fact,

Lotus feet, an old Chinese practice of female foot binding, did not always carry the stigma of female oppression that it does today. Historians in the late 19th century viewed the practice as a cultural idiosyncrasy, an interesting practice to be "noted" rather than a health hazard or form of barbarity. Feminist thinkers in the 20th century, **37** <u>therefore</u>, strongly criticized the practice, calling it inhumane violence by which men imposed absurd standards of beauty upon women.

37

A) NO CHANGE

B) especially,

C) though,

D) indeed,

Circuit City was forced to declare bankruptcy after yet another poor quarterly report. Once one of the giants of electronic retail along with Best Buy, Circuit City cited the rise of online competitors like Ebay and Amazon as the primary reason for its decline. "We have never faltered, **38** <u>likewise,</u> from our goal of treating our customers with respect and dignity," the spokesperson said.

38

A) NO CHANGE

B) moreover,

C) thus,

D) however,

In the documentary *My Life as a Turkey*, Joe Hutto, an ornithologist studying the social hierarchy of wild turkeys, goes into the wild and joins a brood of young turkeys, raising them to adulthood in a course of a year. The birds imprinted on Hutto and followed him around, exhibiting strong loyalty and treating him as a parent. **39** <u>At the same time,</u> when the male turkeys reached adulthood, the male turkeys became threatened by Hutto and treated him as a competitor, eventually going so far as to attack him.

39

A) NO CHANGE

B) On the other hand,

C) For example,

D) Interestingly,

Since its inception, crowdfunding has widened its appeal to consumers. At first, sites like Kickstarter and Indiegogo merely pooled backers' funds to urge proposed products to market. A new crowdsourcing venture like LendingClub, **40** for example, allows its members to freely offer and grant monetary loans at their personalized rates.

40

A) NO CHANGE

B) thus,

C) indeed,

D) on the other hand,

Chapter 4

Diction

Chapter Guide

Diction

Diction questions test your ability to pick the most appropriate word in context. The New SAT avoids especially difficult or obscure words. If you are capable of reading articles from major newspapers, you likely possess adequate vocabulary to do well on these questions.

Because there are impossibly many number of words and unpredictably varying contexts that can appear on the exam, there are no hard and fast rules about diction. However, we can develop a keen sensitivity so that we can evaluate words based on these categories:

1. Formal vs. Informal

Example 1

When the congressman <u>blew off</u> the constituents' repeated attempts to reach him, the public threatened to vote for his challenger in the upcoming election.

A) NO CHANGE
B) ditched
C) gave a cold shoulder to
D) **neglected**

Without reading the underlined portion, try to come up with a prediction based on context. The public is clearly angry about the congressman's behavior, so we can reason that the attempts were *ignored*. *Blow off, ditch,* and *give a cold shoulder to* are informal expressions that should be avoided.

Note that phrasal verbs tend to carry a lighter, colloquial tone.

Example 2

Keeping your daily activities organized on Google Calendar is an effective way of <u>staying on top of</u> your responsibilities.

A) NO CHANGE
B) **managing**
C) staying up-to-date
D) keep up with

2. Positive vs. Negative

Example 1

After following a rigorous diet routine, the ballerina was content with her new, lithe frame; however, her friends expressed concern that she looks <u>graceful</u>.

A) NO CHANGE
B) **malnourished**
C) limber
D) slender

Work with the context clue; *however* indicates that the word we're looking for should be contrasted with the word *lithe*, which means being flexible. Since *graceful* and *limber* are positive words each meaning, *elegant* and *pliant*, eliminate them. *Slender* carries a neutral meaning here, as it means *thin*. Since we need to express the friends' concern *malnourished*, with its negative meaning, is proper.

Example 2

Although Jason, with his thick-rimmed glasses and an immaculate bowtie, appeared <u>well-read</u>, he was actually an extrovert, a truly wild "life of a party."

A) NO CHANGE
B) scholarly
C) erudite
D) **bookish**

Although necessitates a contrast here, and *actually* should provide a context clue. We are looking to find a word that is opposite of the quality possessed by *an extrovert. Well-read* merely means to have read many books. *Scholarly* means dedicated to studious pursuits. *Erudite* means knowledgeable or learned. *Bookish* carries the negative connotation that provides the appropriate contrast.

3. Using root components

Example 1

No discussion about America's quest for racial equality would be complete without the examination of W.E.B. Du Bois and Booker T. Washington, the African-American <u>luminaries</u> of the nineteenth century.

A) **NO CHANGE**
B) celebrities
C) monarchs
D) executives

A *celebrity* is someone who is simply popular and well known. A *monarch* is a king or such ruler. An *executive* is a person who has supervisory authority. While *luminary* has a literal definition of "something that gives light," its more figurative meaning is "someone who has gained eminence in field and serves as an inspiration for others." Therefore, a luminary is a knowledgeable person who leads others. Note that you could use your knowledge of Latin prefix *lum* (light) to infer its meaning.

Example 2

When the stockholders accused the company of misappropriating the funds, the director of the board <u>secluded</u> the topic and pointed at the quarterly report instead.

A) NO CHANGE
B) navigated
C) prevented
D) **circumvented**

Seclude means to cut off. Consider its components *sec* (cut) and *clude* (close). *Navigate* means to move or maneuver, as to travel. *Prevent* means to avert or keep from happening. While it may seem usable, *preventing the topic* results in awkward construction. *Circumvent* means to bypass. Consider its components *circum* (around) and *vent* (go). Alternatively, you can try imagining its related words like *circumlocution, circumspect* to infer its connotation.

Chapter 4

Diction

Practice Questions

Today, we gather to mourn the **1** retired, who perished while valiantly fighting an alligator.

1

A) NO CHANGE
B) evacuated
C) vacated
D) departed

The benefit far **2** outdoes the discomfort of having to wear a seatbelt.

2

A) NO CHANGE
B) defeats
C) outperforms
D) outweighs

The feast **3** satiated the hunger, but it left the partygoers drowsy for the conversation.

3

A) NO CHANGE
B) fulfilled
C) complemented
D) sufficed

While storing compost is a noble endeavor, you should **4** devour it before it stinks up the house!

4

A) NO CHANGE
B) dispatch
C) overindulge
D) dispose of

The pictures of Dust Bowl farmers during the Great Depression feature **5** austere countenances.

5

A) NO CHANGE
B) egregious
C) unmitigated
D) stark

In the US, plumbers and electricians must be **6** decreed in order to operate.

6

A) NO CHANGE
B) commissioned
C) forced
D) licensed

The crime syndicate's plot was **7** confided by the intrepid detective.

7

A) NO CHANGE
B) promulgated
C) imparted
D) unveiled

For the dedicated scientist, his research was **8** emphatic: nothing else mattered.

8

A) NO CHANGE
B) paramount
C) eminent
D) important

After months of **9** tolerating the girl of his dreams, the young man grew tired and weary.

9

A) NO CHANGE
B) pursuing
C) persisting
D) keeping on

The Constitution ensures equal rights to all, regardless of age, sex, race, or sexual **10** orientation.

10

A) NO CHANGE
B) point
C) location
D) direction

The giant rock that fell from the mountain **11** challenges the entrance of the tunnel.

11

A) NO CHANGE
B) impedes
C) obstructs
D) opposes

Despite his age, my grandfather shows great **12** acuteness in vision and hearing.

12

A) NO CHANGE
B) knack
C) prowess
D) astuteness

The dog **13** perpetuated away the bone in the most unlikely spot: inside the refrigerator.

13

A) NO CHANGE

B) stored

C) preserved

D) stashed

If you do not **14** harvest the wound, it will fester!

14

A) NO CHANGE

B) cultivate

C) tend to

D) burgeon

The audience **15** hurled the speaker for his offensive political remarks.

15

A) NO CHANGE

B) spurred

C) heckled

D) launched

"I am but a prodigal son," confessed the gambler, recounting his experience of **16** gambling his father's money.

16

A) NO CHANGE

B) scattering

C) squandering

D) misplacing

When the fire eventually **17** submerged the house, the firefighters worked to secure a viable exit.

17

A) NO CHANGE

B) drowned

C) engulfed

D) sheathed

Some historians argue that South Korea's industrialization was merely **18** communal to President Park Chung-hee's rule, not consequent.

18

A) NO CHANGE

B) congruous

C) conjoint

D) coincident

'The princess' **19** <u>schema</u> was a front: in private, she was quite calculating.

19

A) NO CHANGE

B) naiveté

C) callowness

D) youth

20 <u>Purity</u> in a maiden is a virtue long cherished by patriarchal societies.

20

A) NO CHANGE

B) Spotlessness

C) Clarity

D) Characteristics

The old man was a mere **21** <u>silhouette</u> of his former confident, garrulous self: he lay on his hospital bed all day, staring out the window.

21

A) NO CHANGE

B) shadow

C) likeness

D) lineament

Born with a **22** <u>innocuous</u> gastrointestinal system, the poor man suffered indigestion throughout his life.

22

A) NO CHANGE

B) weak

C) sapless

D) insipid

Capital punishment remains a **23** <u>controversial</u> topic to this day.

23

A) NO CHANGE

B) arguable

C) disputable

D) debatable

A (an) **24** <u>serviceable</u> procedure, the stem cell transplant is not yet widespread in use.

24

A) NO CHANGE

B) empirical

C) experimental

D) practical

Tell me the exact **25** <u>coordination</u>, so I can find you on the map.

25

A) NO CHANGE

B) coordinates

C) disposition

D) displacement

Our picnic plan is in motion; the only **26** <u>variety</u> that may impede it is weather.

26

A) NO CHANGE

B) hiccup

C) agenda

D) variable

Winking is the time-old method of **27** <u>falsely</u> communicating a secret.

27

A) NO CHANGE

B) virtually

C) implicitly

D) expressly

The wife's habit of **28** <u>impulsive</u> shopping annoyed the husband.

28

A) NO CHANGE

B) makeshift

C) impromptu

D) unscripted

Although the young composer fits the stereotype of a **29** <u>reclusive</u> genius, his compositions convey a sense of cosmopolitan sensibility.

29

A) NO CHANGE

B) sequestered

C) restricted

D) sheltered

Although the trail is a sight to behold from afar, actually hiking it is a challenge, for it features **30** <u>vulnerable</u> turns and peaks.

30

A) NO CHANGE

B) malignant

C) susceptible

D) treacherous

To stop the alien monster from bursting through the door, the frightened residents **31** maintained the door with a tall pile of furniture.

31

A) NO CHANGE

B) bolstered

C) endured

D) supported

While many like to hail *Pinocchio* for its lesson in morality, no one asks how Geppetto was able to **32** motivate the initially lifeless doll.

32

A) NO CHANGE

B) animate

C) energize

D) instigate

The outdoor concert was **33** truncated due to an unforeseen power outage.

33

A) NO CHANGE

B) sheared

C) curtailed

D) diminished

Members of the Catholic faith count the prayer beads to **34** inventory earthly sins.

34

A) NO CHANGE

B) enumerate

C) recite

D) compute

The principal **35** excused the students who systematically bullied their underclassmen; he was recognized for his quick, adequate response in the matter.

35

A) NO CHANGE

B) expelled

C) dismissed

D) discharged

The trained archaeologist determined that the hieroglyphs—though badly damaged—were **36** articulated.

36

A) NO CHANGE

B) decipherable

C) meaningful

D) distinct

A (an) **37** questioning mind is able to break down an argument into its logical functions.

37

A) NO CHANGE

B) analytical

C) reasonable

D) detailed

Theories regarding the afterlife must be able to demonstrate the possibility of human existence aside from a **38** material one.

38

A) NO CHANGE

B) corporeal

C) mortal

D) living

Graduating from an Ivy League school has greatly **39** optimized his status.

39

A) NO CHANGE

B) levitated

C) elevated

D) elected

Contrary to the imperialists' expectations, the subjugated people **40** diligently embraced the influx of foreign culture, even adopting some of the customs enthusiastically.

40

A) NO CHANGE

B) emphatically

C) stringently

D) dispassionately

Answer Explanations

Addition/Deletion/Placement

Q	Ans	Explanation
1.	D	The scope of discussion should be limited to the use of DNA to aid criminal investigations, which is the main point of the paragraph. (A) and (C) are simply false statements. (B) shifts the focus to the "study of DNA," which is broader than the intended scope.
2.	D	**Key word: however** The transition word, "however," necessitates a contrasting precedent statement. Sentences [4] and [5] discuss how difficult it was to be on screen "in the past." Since sentence [2] discusses today's relative ease of broadcasting, it should come after sentence [5].
3.	C	The passage details the qualities that made da Vinci the "epitome of the Renaissance Man." The underlined sentence does provide details about da Vinci, but it's irrelevant to the topic of the Renaissance Man. (D) may seem attractive, but details about his birth or education are not exactly statements about his childhood.
4.	D	Always consider the scope. The passage discusses the problems associated with trendy diets. Whether men are also attracted to trendy diets is not relevant within the scope of the passage, so (B) should be eliminated. (C) is incorrect because the sentence does not counter the main point: that trendy diets are vicious traps. (A) cannot be justified as it fails to support this argument.
5.	D	**Key word: transparency** The keyword "transparency," which appears in the first sentence, is a topic that is explored later in the paragraph. Sentence [1] is the general claim. Sentences [3] and [4] provide detail by explaining what exactly is transparent about the way the restaurant operates. Sentence [2] brings up the "pricey" dishes and introduces the owner. Therefore, the best placement would be after the discussion of menu prices and before the quoted statement by the owner.
6.	A	**Key phrase: This development** "This development" is a phrase that requires an antecedent. Sentence [3] discusses a new trend in consumption.
7.	A	**Key phrase: not a luxury afforded to the poor** The main claim in the passage is that the woman who posed for Mona Lisa is likely someone who was wealthy. While the underlined sentence provides support to the claim, it does not provide an actual statistic that is explored further, so (B) can be eliminated. (C) should be considered; however, the last sentence makes a clear contrast between the poor and the wealthy. Therefore, the underlined sentence serves an important function in the passage.
8.	B	**Key phrase: popularize its appeal** Sentence [5] is a general statement about Louis Armstrong's contribution — that he popularized improvisation. Sentence [2] elaborates on the popularity, by describing Armstrong "a sensation of the music halls."

9.	A	**Key words: critics, proponents, however** The passage proceeds by describing the new law, the critics' response, and the proponents' response. The addition would make a smooth transition between the critics' response and the proponents' response, because of the transition word "however."
10.	C	**Key word: cooperation** Stated in another way, Sentence [5] says that the EPA works with others. Sentence [3] lays out a condition that the EPA's work requires cooperation with other parties. Note that although Sentence [2] does introduce "policymakers," the relationship is adversarial rather than cooperative.
11.	D	Be careful; the main point here is not that "Korean fried chicken is popular everywhere." The passage is narrowly focused on the increased consumption in Korea, so there is no reason to broaden the scope to include fried chicken's "international appeal." Also note that the last sentence is not meant to elevate Korea's chicken consumption to an international phenomenon; it merely notes that the number of franchise restaurants has surpassed the number of another easily-identified marker of popularity.
12.	C	The scope of discussion should be limited to the signing of a new law, the circumstances leading to its signing, and its effect. A statement describing the local residents' affinity towards a particular book expands the scope and detracts from the discussion of the law itself.
13.	C	**Key phrase: the study** Sentence [1] introduces "a study," and Sentence [2] summarizes its finding. Sentence [5] elaborates on the main claim. Note that Sentences [4], [6], and [7] discuss different brain parts and are inseparably linked.
14.	A	**Key phrases: some lament, proponents argue** Sentences [1] through [4] discuss automation of labor as a new phenomenon. Sentence [5] summarizes the viewpoint of some who believe that automation is a loss. Sentence [6] provides contrast, which is supported by Sentence [7].
15.	C	**Key phrases: for example, stimulate, elevate** Since Sentences [1] and [2] are a question and its corresponding answer, they are inseparable. Sentence [3] calls an example of "stimulating" into the discussion and therefore must be preceded by a general statement. Sentence [5] is a general statement, and "elevating" is an idea elaborated by "stimulate."
16.	B	**Key phrases: improved retention, in order to, these areas, this program, issues of retention, the program** Sentence [1] introduces the problem that remote and rural areas are having. Sentence [3] elaborates on the problem and discusses what a potential solution may be. Sentences [2], [4], and [5] introduce a program that seeks to improve retention of health workers. Note the use of pronouns like "these," "this," and the definite article "the." These words function as hint words that can tell us the sequence of the sentences.
17.	C	The passage discusses the difficulty of launching an online shopping mall; the scope is the difficulty in relation to cybersecurity. The underlined sentence introduces potential reasons why launching an online shopping mall may be difficult. Indeed, "competition" and "turnover rates" are hurdles for a new entrepreneur. Unfortunately, they do not relate to cybersecurity and is therefore irrelevant. Note (A) and (D) mention cybersecurity but misconstrue the main point.

18.	C	**Key phrases: seated in the reception area, arduous, though** By Sentence [3], the narrator is seated with a numbered ticket. It follows that he or she would be able to interact with others who were sitting after that. Note that Sentence [4] has a contrast word "though." Since the wait was arduous (a negative experience), it can stand as the logical contrast to the positive experience with the accommodating lady at the window.
19.	D	The focus of discussion is on the beneficial effects of music education. The sentence we want to add introduces Mozart, who, despite being a historically well known compositional genius, says nothing about music education here. Take care not to deduce or infer information.
20.	A	(B) is false, because listing the kinds of distractions does not directly support the argument that all devices should be banned. Just mentioning "online VODs" does not necessarily discuss students' online activities; eliminate (D). You should weigh (A) and (C). Because the last sentence discusses "electronic devices," it would be a good idea to mention the specific types early on in the paragraph. Since the discussion leads with the advancement of technology, electronic devices have immediate relevance to the paragraph.
21.	A	(B) may sound good, because it correctly states the main point of the passage. However, the given sentence introduces two new methods rather than provide evidence of innovation. "Whistleblowers" and "call for change" are relevant phrases in discussing political activism, so eliminate (C). The legality of the methods of digital activism is not the focus of the passage, so even if (D) were true, it cannot be the answer.
22.	B	**Key phrase: reevaluated their curricula** Sentences [1] and [2] discuss Dr. Gardner's new theory, so they should not be separated. Sentences [3] and [4] are related because they elaborate on the schools' responses to Dr. Gardner's findings.
23.	C	**Key phrases: the Los Angeles Times, the critics, other publications.** Sentence [1] introduces a single critic, the Los Angeles Times, yet Sentence [2] introduces multiple critics. This is why you should pay special attention to things like pronouns, articles, and plurality. By introducing the "other publications," you can safely refer to them as "the critics."
24.	D	The passage, as a whole, is describing the life cycle of a cicada. Note the sequential construction of the passage. The given sentence, however, reorients the discussion to the role of climate change on the cicada life cycle. You could consider (A) since it is true; however, the last sentence elaborates on molting, so it would result in needless shifts in topic.
25.	C	The underlined sentence defines a term attributed to Anderson. The phrase "pastel-colored sets and soundtracks" provides how Anderson controls all (visual and auditory) aspects of the film. (A) is not true; the definition of an auteur is not a restatement of the critics' favorable opinion. Since the first sentence introduces the subject and the underlined sentence elaborates, they flow logically; eliminate (B). (D) is not true; critics' holding in high regard is unrelated to Anderson's approach as an auteur.
26.	A	(B) makes an unnecessary inference; "breaking with the conservative paradigm" does not make claim of a particular political affiliation. Likewise, there is no evidence the filmmakers were "unhappy"; eliminate (C). (D) misconstrues the main point of the passage.
27.	D	**Key phrases: alarmist rhetoric, the alarmists, needless to say** Sentence [3] introduces an alarmist rhetoric, so those who espouse it must be the alarmists! Sentence [5] quotes the alarmists and therefore serves as an elaboration of Sentence [3]. The phrase "needless to say" introduces a summary, and it sums up the baselessness of the alarmists' worry, closing the paragraph.

28.	C	**Key phrases: these perennial questions, less known, however, common knowledge** Sentences [1] and [2] are "these questions" referred to in Sentence [3] and therefore can't be separated. There is a contrast between "less known" and "common knowledge." Note Sentence [6] serves as an elaboration of the less known instances of physical abuse in Sentence [4].
29.	C	(A) is simply false; there is no transition to animal gifs. The paragraph's focus is on the author's argument, not the number of gifs online, so (B) is incorrect. (D) is unrelated to the main point of the paragraph, and is not a valid reason.
30.	D	The underlined sentence merely provides one of distinguishing features of Murakami's works, but it is not an emphasis of a particular feature; eliminate (B). (C) is clearly inaccurate; there is no personal life discussed. (A) and (D) could be true. With a careful reading, you should see that the last sentence is a reformulation of the second reason. "Using fantastical elements to stimulate" is essentially the same as "strange, mysterious plots readers feel compelled to read."
31.	B	(A) is inaccurate, and (D) offers no support why something is "inappropriate." Eliminate them. (B) and (C) are true statements. When faced with multiple true statements in addition questions, ask if what the choice says is necessary. In (C), while it's true the given sentence does not provide a detailed statistic in numbers, it is a claim sentence; it is not necessary to provide statistics in it.
32.	A	**Key phrases: career prospects, choose to be a scholar** Sentence [5] elaborates on the problem of career availability introduced in Sentence [1].
33.	C	"Working relationships," and "actively engage" are phrases related to networking, or forging connections. The previous sentence uses a strong verb "need" in order to emphasize the importance of networking. Therefore, there is no need to repeat this claim again within the paragraph.
34.	D	**Key phrases: talent to succeed, in addition, a successful blogger must be** Sentence [4] makes a transition to discuss the requirements to be a blogger. Note the indefinite article "a" in Sentence [6], and the pronouns "he or she" in Sentence [5]. Logically, you should introduce an indefinite blogger first before referring to him or her using pronouns. Contextually, Sentence [4] is the claim; Sentence [6] is the support, and Sentence [5] is additional support.
35.	C	(D) can be eliminated since the underlined sentence is not a conclusion. (B) is similarly false; the sentence did not mention genes at all. (A) is incorrect because the sentence does not repeat information. The underlined sentence is a definition of a term marked with quotation marks. The use of quotation marks indicates that the author is introducing a technical term in need of elaboration. Therefore, the underlined sentence cannot be "unnecessary."
36.	C	**Key phrases: Like the tuba, however, unlike the tuba** Sentences [2] and [4] are definition and origin of the sousaphone, respectively. Sentence [4] discusses sousaphones maneuverability, while Sentence [5] transitions to the method of projection. Since there is a logical contrast between the similarity to a tuba and the dissimilarity to a tuba, Sentences [3] and [6] belong together.
37.	D	The main point of the passage is that lighter skin is more prone to damage. Because melanin is responsible for tanning and tanning prevents damage, the definition of melanin is an important detail that should be included. Eliminate (A) and (B) because they are false. While (C) could be true, whether melanin causes cancer is not the focus of the passage.

38.	C	"Similar deals" should offer a clue here. Because the last sentence relies on a previous example, it is necessary to include Clark Kent's method of hiding his identity. (A) is false, because the scope of the passage is larger than Clark Kent. (B) is false, because it is a relevant detail. (D) is false, because the "kind" of employment is not the focus of the discussion.
39.	A	The topic of the passage is the Mozart Effect; the passage discusses its impact on IQ testing and the subsequent influence on policy. Introducing a certain type of IQ test is out of scope.
40.	D	**Key phrases: prohibitive costs, will be able to afford, lower the cost of production, such countries.** Sentences [1] and [2] introduce the 3D printing and its potentially beneficial applications. Sentences [3] and [4] introduce a problem (production is too expensive!). Sentence [5] discusses the potential benefit conferred. Since the given sentence elaborates on how 3D printing can lower costs, it should come between Sentences [4] and [5].

Sentence Combinations

Q	Ans	Explanation
1.	D	The second sentence defines a technical term "antiphonal structure." Nonessential back modifier "which" does the job here. (A) "Which means that" is a wordy construction. Avoid it. (B) "Moreover" is illogical; we're not trying to give further information. (C) "Because" is illogical; there is no causal relationship in the sentences.
2.	C	(A) "A group of composers" and "it" are repeating subjects that could be consolidated. (B) "In the early 20th century" is better placed up front. Also, "arose" was never used in the original sentences, was it? Be wary of choices that change meanings. (D) Passive voice used here makes the choice wordy. "Did so" is redundant here.
3.	A	Just by adding a colon, the two sentences are combined. Remember that a colon is used to provide additional detail that either restates or explains the first independent clause. Based on context, we want to explain why the headset would be an innovative gadget. (B) changes the meaning. (C) "Innovative" is the focus of discussion here. Do not separate it off as an nonessential modifier. (D) may look attractive due to its concision, but it switches the focus onto the availability of the entertainment system, rather than why it's innovative.
4.	B	(A), (B), and (C) are all grammatically correct and mean the same thing. You should prefer the most concise choice. (A) is Independent Clause (IC), Coordinating Conjunction (CC) + IC, and (C) has two separate sentences. (D), while concise, cannot work here because "omniscience" is not "a feeling of unease."
5.	D	This is a concision question; choice (D) offers the most straightforward description of the similarity between "writers" and "painters."
6.	A	Make sure back modifiers work with the context provided by the first sentence. The correct choice should describe "stealing" what Vanilla Ice was accused of doing. (B) "Tried to" is wordy. (C) separates the two ideas; we want them to flow together! (D) "by which" is inappropriate here.
7.	C	(A), (B), (C) are all grammatically correct and mean the same thing. You should prefer the most concise choice. (D) introduces "such that," which means "to the extent that" and is illogical here.
8.	D	Remember that Sentence Combination questions are looking for fewer S-V relationships in the correct choice. Front or back modifiers are generally preferred. (A) and (B) essentially mean the same thing, and grammatically they have two independent clauses. (C) looks good; however, (D) is more concise.

9.	C	(A) and (C) offer contextually appropriate sentences. Go with the more concise (C). "Because" is wrong in (B), and (D) uses "being" inappropriately.
10.	C	The first sentence introduces "wide-ranging physical disciplines," and the second sentence elaborates what they are by listing three individual activities. (A) is grammatically incorrect, because "many of which" results in a dependent clause. Although (B) is a concise form that has one S-V relationship, it changes the meaning of the sentence and does not elaborate on the wide-ranging disciplines. (D) changes the meaning of the sentence.
11.	D	Note that there is a contrast between "modestly" and "luster of regal dignity." The first sentence says the throne room is plainly decorated; the second sentence provides a contrast, saying some components were shiny and fancy. (A) and (B) do not introduce contrast. Eliminate them. (C) is a decent choice, but the possessive adjective pronoun "its" is required to provide the full context.
12.	B	Smartphones rob attention, harm eyesight, and take up a lot of free time. The correct choice must introduce these details in a concise manner. Note "robbing attention" and "taking up free time" are related ideas that work together. "What make smartphones dangerous" adds a meaning not in the original sentences. It is also wordy. Eliminate (A). (B) misplaces "robbing" and "harmful." (D) fails to connect "robbing attention" with "taking up time."
13.	A	Remember to eliminate choices that contain grammatical errors first. (C) results in Independent Clause (IC), IC; eliminate it. (B) and (D) introduce the subordinating conjunction "because," which is inappropriate here.
14.	A	Note that "the California Gold Rush of 1849" is the event, and "a massive settlement" is the description that belongs to it. (B) inverts the relationship by introducing the em dashes. In (C), "the adventurers" cannot be equated to a massive settlement. (D) is wrong grammatically and contextually. Remember you need a comma to separate two independent clauses joined by a coordinating conjunction.
15.	A	In (B) the entrance guarantees; based on context, it should be the closed-circuit camera and an alarm system that do so. (D) introduces the subordinating conjunction "since"; it is not logical to include here. We are left with (A) and (C), which mean the same thing. When left with choices that mean the same, always prefer back modifiers to full independent clauses.
16.	C	In (A), "still" has no reason to be there. (B) introduces "however," which is illogical here as there is no contrast. In (D), "wasn't having to" is erroneous. The verb "have to" may not be presented in progressive forms.

17.	B	The second sentence wants to elaborate on the shoppers; use the relative pronoun "who" to give further detail. (A) is contextually inappropriate. Note (C) introduces a coordinating conjunction after a semicolon. The preferred punctuation here would be a comma.
18.	C	The sentences provide a clear contrast between "some lawyers" and "other lawyers." While (A) is grammatically correct, it fails to connect the sentences in a logically precise manner. (B) and (C) mean the same thing; always prefer the concise constructions. In (D), the colon is inappropriate here, as we are not providing an explanation for the first part of the sentence.
19.	C	The question asks to elaborate upon the figure "1 million SHU." Using a relative pronoun clause is an acceptable option here, so keep (A). However, using an em dash accomplishes the same function. Go with the concise choice. (B) introduces "therefore," which is illogical here. (D) is identical to (A) and (C) in meaning, but it is wordier than both.
20.	D	"Day in and day out" and "until life becomes…" are both modifying phrases that can work with the initial independent clause. In (A) "which they do" is unnecessary because it is merely restating "dwell" and "enumerate." Similarly, in (B), "which means" adds unnecessary interpretation to an otherwise concise idea. (C) introduces "although," which is illogical.
21.	A	All choices are grammatically acceptable. This means you should evaluate the choices based on logic or context, then concision. Note there is a contrast (negative vs. positive). Playing the guitar becomes more difficult, but the sound is thicker and smoother. Eliminate (C) and (D) for illogical transition words. (B) misplaces the conjunctive adverb "however."
22.	C	Read the sentences carefully. The second sentence explains the reason why Korea gained momentum. The "unparalleled success" came first, and it resulted in Korea's "gaining momentum." (A) does not make this relationship explicit. (D) reverses the order. While (B) and (C) may look identical in meaning, the main thought in (B) is that "Korea was propelled," because "gaining momentum" is a nonessential modifier. Front modifier as an introductory phrase works here, because it sets up the condition "propelled" before describing the result, "gained momentum."
23.	D	Because all choices are grammatically acceptable, evaluate them based on logic and context, then on concision. (B) is the easiest to eliminate; "because" is illogical here. (A) is identical to the original sentences, save for "after that." Of course the disciples will use the theory after its formation. Look for a better option. (C) looks okay, since it uses a back modifier "which." However, it is wordy on two counts. "Which they applied" and "in order to" should be shortened further. Worse still, it changes the focus of the sentences from "applying" to "were influenced."
24.	B	(D) should be eliminated because "disappeared" and "missing" are redundant. (A), (B), and (C) are all grammatically acceptable and essentially mean the same; in such cases, always prefer the most concise choice.

25.	A	Let's eliminate grammatically wrong choices first. In (B) "in order to reduced" is inaccurate usage. (C) results in a comma splice (Independent Clause, Independent Clause). (A) and (D) are grammatically acceptable, but (D) is clearly wordier.
26.	D	(A) is grammatically acceptable, so keep it for now. "Hence" means "therefore." Eliminate (C) for illogical construction. (B) and (D) essentially mean the same. Opt for the more concise option.
27.	C	In the paragraph, there is a contrast between a method of messaging called "IM" and its more recent name "texting." Eliminate (A) and (B) because these do not introduce contrast. "But" and "whereas" may seem similar but are used quite differently. Use "but" for extreme contrast between subjects, and use "whereas" for comparison in a manner similar to "while."
28.	C	Note the comparison between "the common name" and "the Japanese nomenclature." "Whereas" is the only word that introduces comparison here.
29.	D	"The Rite of Spring" is referred as "the piece." This type of question asks for an elaboration on the last noun of the first sentence. (A) changes the meaning. (C) introduces an illogical transition word, "yet." (B) and (D) mean the same. Opt for the more concise choice.
30.	D	Note the redundancy. As the theory predicted, the elementary particles and atoms both possess wave-like characters. The characters were verified, confirming the predictions. (C) is the easiest to eliminate; "although" is illogical here. (A), (C), and (D) mean the same. Always prefer the most concise choice.
31.	D	The second independent clause should elaborate on the noun, "goal." Eliminate (C), because the coordinating conjunction "for" is illogical. (A), (B), and (D) all elaborate on "goal." Always prefer the most concise choice.
32.	C	The best choice will identify the causal relationship between the sentences. Reagan possessed certain qualities, and they were the reason why he won the election. (A) shifts the focus to "was known for." (B) is illogical; the reason for Reagan's victory was his qualities, not that his qualities were known. In (D), whether Reagan himself knew of his own qualities is immaterial to the focus. We should keep the ideas concise. Introduce the cause with a front modifier "known," and close with the effect.
33.	B	It's a good idea to join these sentences together. Note "it" here would be an ambiguous pronoun. (D) repeats this error; eliminate it. (A) and (C) introduce illogical transition words.

| 34. | D | Double check the commas' locations!

The phrase "thanks to the new technology" should introduce a positive idea.

(A) is grammatically unacceptable; "thanks to" phrase is not an independent clause and may not follow a semicolon.

(C) results in a comma splice.

Eliminate (B) because based on context, "thanks to" phrase should belong to the second idea, not the first. |
|---|---|---|
| 35. | B | Be careful! Though (C) and (D) may look attractive, context comes before concision. "A biting criticism on theism" cannot be equated to "an atheist's defense." Therefore, he must be offering two different things in his book. (A) is missing a subject and a verb. |
| 36. | B | First, eliminate (C) for grammar. Without a comma after "mind," the verb "gathered" cannot agree with the subjects.

(A), (B), and (D) essentially mean the same. There is no reason to use an em dash here, because the verb "gathered" and the adverb "clandestinely" should be joined without an intervening punctuation. |
| 37. | A | "Mark Zuckerberg" is the proper subject here, and "the founder and CEO" should be nonessential modifier.

(B) adds a wordy relative pronoun clause.

(C) changes the subject to "belief" and thus results in a focus shift.

In (D), since "who" is introduced without a comma, it is an essential modifier. It's grammatically acceptable, but it is contextually not. |
| 38. | C | Note the cause and effect relationship here. "Kafka's astute observation" works as the cause, and the "coining" is the effect.

Eliminate (B) for grammar, because there is no independent clause after the semicolon.

In (A), "leading" is inadequate as a verb, because the "coining" was only the result, not something that was actively led to.

In (D), without a comma between "circles" and "leading," the back modifier becomes essential and can only describe the word "circles," instead of the entire independent clause. |
| 39. | C | The dumping occurred in Boston, MA. Samuel Adams defended the dumping.

(A) does not address the repetition of the word "dumping."

(B) omits Samuel Adams as one responsible for "defending."

(D) states that the "defending" took place in Boston, MA; the dumping did.

Note that in (C), the relative pronoun "which" can describe the word "dumping," thanks to the precedent comma. |

40.	A	Eliminate (C) for unnecessary punctuation. A colon is not needed between a noun and an essential modifier following it. (A), (B), and (D) mean the same thing. Eliminate (D) because Independent Clause; Independent Clause is the wordiest among the three. (B) introduces a relative clause back modifier, which is wordier than (A).

Transition

Q	Ans	Explanation
1.	C	**Example** The second sentence gives an example of the revolutionary ways that the app users can utilize the service.
2.	B	**Result** The admiral's last words "bolstered" the soldiers' morales, which inspired them to fight courageously.
3.	B	**Contrast** "Online postings" are contrasted with "a handwritten notice." "Inundated with application" is contrasted with "may go unnoticed." "Corporate jobs" are contrasted with a position for a "small bakery."
4.	A	**Addition** The paragraph discusses the way in which the wealthy could use new technology to "oppress." The last sentence gives additional ways in which the oppression can take form. Note that furtherance of an idea should not be introduced with "thus."
5.	C	**Example** A general statement about YouTube's contribution is followed by a more specific case of "one prominent videographer."
6.	B	**Time** "Consequently" or "as a result" would work wonderfully here, since the authors of the study is acting as a result of the findings. However, since no result-related transition word is given, go with one that does not violate the logical relationship of ideas. There is no example, contrast, or similarity between the ideas. Eliminate (A), (C), and (D).
7.	B	**Emphasis** Note that (C) and (D) can seem appealing; however, the last sentence is an affirmation that raising wage has been a difficult process, rather than a claim that labor unions achieved higher wages through their struggles. Alternatively, you could rule out (C) and (D) for being synonymous in this context.
8.	D	**Contrast** "Incompetent" is contrasted with "actually well qualified."

#		
9.	D	**Result** Note "then" can be both time-related or showing conclusion. Here, the previous descriptions of the Fourth Industrial Revolution lead the author to conclude its potential impact.
10.	A	**Result** The author argues that the "nature's warnings" should lead us to "support the environmentalists." Since there is evidence and a resulting action,
11.	D	**Result** "Accordingly" means "in a way that is appropriate to circumstance just described" and is similar to "consequently" or "therefore."
12.	D	A result-related transition word could have worked here. But (A) introduces addition, (B) introduces time, and (C) introduces contrast. Using this process of elimination, only (D) results in a logically consistent sentence.
13.	B	**Contrast** "Most students were overjoyed" is contrasted with "others... worried"
14.	C	**Purpose** "To this end" means "in order to achieve a particular aim." Marsalis' interpretation argues that certain elements of the music must be "preserved." The last sentence describes how neoclassicists try to accomplish this goal.
15.	B	In some cases, the best transition defines the range of discussion rather than confines it with logic. (A) and (D) are usable, but time is not of importance here. (C) introduces something to be contrasted, but is unacceptable without completing the contrast.
16.	C	**Example** The last sentence provides an example of the No Gadget policy in action.
17.	C	**Summary** The paragraph introduces two ideas about the Socratic method: it is popular, but it has its critics. The last sentence is a restatement of the main point of the paragraph. Though (B) may look attractive, it introduces an ambiguous pronoun. What does it mean by "this," exactly? (A) and (D) are synonymous, so you must be cautious. While "consequently" and "therefore" may be used to summarize an idea, there must be an idea that led to the natural conclusion. Because the sentence summarizes the whole paragraph rather than the critics' argument, "in other words" is better suited here.
18.	A	**Contrast** The positive effects of increased income is contrasted with the idea that it may not lead to happiness.
19.	A	**Addition** "Cosmetically pleasing and more hygienic" are positive descriptions of the new braces. The last sentence continues the description with its "cost effectiveness."
20.	D	**Contrast** "Typically... during the winter time" is contrasted with "September."

21.	C	**Addition** The paragraph describes the dormitory and its provisions. The last sentence adds "soundproof walls" to the list of provisions.
22.	C	**Example** The paragraph discusses the unexpectedly insightful nature of cryptozoology. The discovery of the gorilla is cited as an example of the fruitful nature of the discipline.
23.	B	**Addition** The paragraph is concerned with voters' approval. In the first sentence, the voters generally disapprove of the Congress' job. In the second sentence, they also disapprove of the President's job.
24.	A	**Result** "A considerable hike on the prices" naturally lead to the customers' dissatisfaction.
25.	D	**Example** "Watching the passersby" is an example of "outdoor activities" that the author was expecting.
26.	C	**Contrast** The larger ants' role is to "scare off" the smaller pests. "The trees grow unhindered" is contrasted with "the trees may turn completely barren."
27.	B	**Addition** The critics argue that cold brew coffee lacks complexity. This negative evaluation is in addition to "a major flaw" introduced by the lack of bitterness.
28.	C	**Contrast** "Some species" are contrasted with "others." Though (A) may look attractive, "alternatively" is used when there are acceptable choices to be made. There is no indication that the organisms are making a choice here.
29.	B	**Contrast** There is a betrayal of expectation here. Though Dali made radical statements, the purpose was not "to show true convictions" but "to inspire shock."
30.	D	**Emphasis** "In fact" is used to emphasize the truth of an assertion, especially in contrast to what has been said or expected. There is an expectation that network routers should be fast. While (B) looks attractive, the contrast is secondary to the emphasis here, since the preceding sentence casts doubt on the routers' performance.
31.	C	**Example** The first sentence lays out a claim, and the second sentence provides the detail that supports the general argument. (A) should be avoided because it puts the claim and the detail on an equal level of importance.
32.	A	**Result** The preceding sentence lays out tasks a chef must be able to perform. The last sentence summarizes the tasks as a requirement.

33.	D	**Emphasis** In the second sentence, the "ubiquitous cultural status" is reinforced by the discussion of K-pop's popularity.
34.	A	**Contrast** There is a contrast between the idea that Freud's assertions being "discredited" but "remaining" elsewhere.
35.	B	**Contrast** The paragraph discusses the change in affordability of leading a bohemian lifestyle. There is a contrast between "400 dollars a month," a presumably affordable amount, and "800 dollars a month," a significantly more expensive sum.
36.	B	**Example** The last sentence provides a specific way Michelle Obama "followed suit." While (D) might be an acceptable choice, the paragraph's progression from a general statement to a specific action taken should disqualify (D) from being the best choice.
37.	C	**Contrast** The paragraph offers a contrast between the "historians in the late 19th century" and "feminist thinkers in the 20th century."
38.	D	**Contrast** The spokesperson's statement contrasts with the expectation of the public. By issuing a statement of defense, the spokesperson seeks to avoid the charge that its poor performance was necessitated by a similarly poor treatment of its customers.
39.	D	While (B) may sound attractive, note that "on the other hand" is used to convey a contrasting point of view. While there is a contrast between "exhibiting loyalty and treating him as a parent" and "became threatened and treated him as competition," it is not a statement of differing perspectives. In (A) "At the same time" should introduce another fact that should be taken into consideration.It is not a support of a general statement, so eliminate (C) as well. The only neutral expression that merely notes the nature of the sudden change, then, is (D).
40.	D	**Contrast** There is a contrast between "merely pooling backers' funds" to "allowing its members to freely offer." This type of contrast is also a statement of comparison between "sites like Kickstarter and Indiegogo" and "a new crowdsourcing venture like LendingClub. In such cases, "on the other hand" is appropriate.

Diction

Q	Ans	Explanation
1.	D	Though "depart" means to leave, **the departed** means one who has died. Consider the contextual clues "mourn" and "perished."
2.	D	**Outweigh** means to exceed in importance or value. "Outdo" and "outperform" mean to do better than. "Defeat" means to beat.
3.	A	"Satiate" means to satisfy a lack. "Fulfill" means carry out to complete a requirement or wish. "Suffice" means to be just enough to satisfy a condition. "Complement" means to complete and is therefore the farthest in meaning. Since hunger is a lack and not a requirement, **satiate** should be preferred.
4.	D	"Devour" means to consume. "Dispatch" means to send out or kill. "Overindulge" means to allow for or promote excess. Let's think with some common sense and **dispose**, or throw out, the compost.
5.	A	"Egregious" means especially bad. "Unmitigated" means unweakened or lessened. Consider "unmitigated damage." "Stark" means utter, clear. **Austere** could mean "stringent or harsh" or "simple." Since these farmers suffering economically, they would look tough yet resigned to the difficulty of life.
6.	D	"Decree" means formally declare or let known. "Commission" means to order. Com (with) + mission (duty). **Licensed** has the correct connotation of passing a requirement here.
7.	D	"Confide" means to tell a secret in trust. Con (with) + fide (belief, trust). "Promulgate" is similar to "decree." It means to let known by declaration. "Impart" means to let known, as well, but it has a connotation of "bestowing. Think of a helpful mentor imparting life wisdom. **Unveiled** carries a connotation of revealing, as to expose. It fits the context here, since the "detective" is someone who would piece together to expose the "plot."
8.	B	Prediction based on context should be "the most important." "Emphatic" means passionate. "Eminent" means of distinguished esteem. **Paramount** means important above everything. Para (beyond) + mount (upward). It is used to describe something that is beyond important in priority.
9.	B	Prediction based on context should be "chasing after" or "following." "Tolerate" means to forgive. "Persist" means to exist continuously. "Keep on" means to continue. It is potentially usable but is not specific enough. Continuing about what? **Pursue** means to chase in order to achieve or attain.

10.	A	"Orient," as a verb, carries the sense of "position" without any ambiguity. Example: 'studies of locational awareness and orientation in young children' In context, **orientation** means one's preference. Direction is incorrect because it indicates movement or guidance.
11.	C	Prediction based on context should be "block." "Impede" means to hinder. Im (against) + ped (foot). Think of someone holding onto a foot that wants to move onward. "Oppose" means to be against in a general sense. **Obstruct** means literally to block, with the figurative meaning closer to "halt" or "interfere." Ob (against) + struct (build).
12.	A	"Knack" means a clever skill or talent. "Prowess" means one's aptitude or skill. "Astuteness" means quality of being wise or keen. **Acuteness** means sharpness or severity.
13.	D	The preposition "away" should serve as a clue here. "Perpetuated away" or "preserved away" are incompatible constructions. Since there is a connotation of "hiding," **stash** is the best option.
14.	C	Harvest means to gather crops. Prediction based on context should be "address" or "deal with." **Tend to** is the only choice with applicable meaning. Cultivate means to grow plants or certain skills or nurture good character.
15.	C	Prediction based on context should be "criticized" or "disapproved." "Hurl" means to throw; throwing the speaker is certainly possible, but it results in an extreme, cartoonish scenario. "Spur" means to goad or to cause to act. **Heckle** means to bother or harass.
16.	C	"Scattering" is easily avoided here, but what about the others? "Gambling" and "misplacing" both result in lost money. However, the context clue is "prodigal," meaning wasteful. **Squander** means to waste and is therefore the most appropriate.
17.	C	"Submerge" means to be under water. "Drown" means to die under water or to flood. "Sheathe" means to cover as a sheath of a sword does, i.e. for concealment. **Engulf** means to swallow or immerse. Note, "drowned in flames" or "engulfed in flames" are in use. However, since we are looking for a verb, **engulf** with its general connotation of swallowing should be preferred, as "drown" implies presence of water.
18.	D	"Communal" means relating to a community. The communal study area is open to students only. "Congruous" means exhibiting harmony. "Conjoint" means joined together. Since we're looking to contrast the word "consequent," **coincident**, which means happening at the same time, is appropriate. Industrialization happened, but it was not directly caused by the President; it merely coincided.
19.	B	"Schema" means a plan or a diagram (of a plan). "Callowness" means a state of being inexperienced. While "callowness" could work, we must contrast with the context clue "calculating." Therefore, **naiveté**, which means being natural, simple, and artless, is appropriate here.

20.	A	"Characteristics" is too broad and unfocused; eliminate it. "Spotlessness" might be a virtue, but the meaning is not clear without context. Similarly, "clarity" results in an ambiguous construction. **Purity**, which means a quality of being unspoiled, is a specific character that renders the sentence coherence.
21.	B	"Silhouette" means an outline of an object. "Likeness" means resemblance. "Lineaments" refers to a facial feature. **Shadow** completes the idiomatic expression "mere shadow of x," meaning "nothing more than."
22.	B	"Innocuous" means harmless. "Sapless" means drained of vitality, either/both physically or mentally. "Insipid" means vapid or uninteresting. A simple **weak**, with its general connotation, will do here.
23.	A	"Controversial" means subject to controversy, as in vigorous debate or speculation. "Arguable" has a positive connotation and offers a possibility of a different interpretation. It is arguable that the team's loss was actually a boon in disguise. "Disputable" has a negative connotation and casts doubt. His claim to truth is disputable, considering his dubious character. "Debatable" is more flexible; based on context it could be construed as positive or negative. In this case, since we are modifying a noun "topic," we are looking for a neutral (neither positive nor negative), general modifier. **Controversial** is the most appropriate.
24.	C	"Serviceable" means adequate in achieving an end. "Empirical" means pertaining to an experience or data. "Practical" means usable in ordinary situations. **Experimental** correctly captures the uncertain nature of the procedure.
25.	B	"Disposition" means tendency or preference. "Displacement" means the moving something by adding something in its place. "Coordination" and "Coordinates" both come from Co (together) + order. "Coordination" means working together. **Coordinates** means particular points, especially on graphs or maps.
26.	D	"Variety" means being varied or diverse. "Agenda" means a plan. **Variable** means an unknown — something that may or may not change. "Hiccup," aside from the pulsing diaphragm, can mean a variable or an unforeseen interference; however, choosing will result in colloquialism.
27.	C	Prediction based on context should be "secretly" or "subtly." "Virtually" means nearly. "Expressly" means explicitly or boldly.
28.	A	"Makeshift" means improvised or assembled together in haste. "Impromptu" means unplanned. "Unscripted" means not written. **Impulsive**, which means swayed by a whim, correctly describes the wife's habit of shopping.

29.	A	"Sequestered" means cut off from society. "Restricted" means limited by imposition. "Sheltered" means protected from troubles. **Reclusive**, which means withdrawn, captures the voluntary solitude that artists are commonly associated with.
30.	D	"Vulnerable" means prone to harm. "Malignant" means likely to cause harm. The malignant cancer cells were surgically removed. "Susceptible" means liable or subject to influence. **Treacherous** has two meanings. It could mean violating faith or betraying. It could also mean simply unstable or dangerous.
31.	B	"Maintain" means to keep in existence. "Endure" means to put up with. "Support" has a general connotation of helping, which is too broad here. **Bolster** means to support, especially by adding something. Note its figurative usage as well. The author bolstered his argument by citing factual evidence.
32.	B	Prediction based on context should be "move" or "give life to." "Motivate" means to give reason for action. "Energize" means to give energy. "Instigate" means to force an action. **Animate** means to make move. "Instigate" is too strong, while "motivate" and "energize" do not correctly describe how a lifeless doll started to move.
33.	A	"Shear" means to cut, in the sense of using a pair of shears to trim. "Curtail" means to cut short, with an added connotation of "restricting." After a serious warning from the doctor, the patient curtailed his habit of smoking. "Diminish" means to reduce in strength or importance. Compared to "curtail" **truncated** carries a more general connotation of "shorten the duration of."
34.	B	"Inventory" is more applicable to checking stocks of items. "Recite" means to repeat the words of, especially from memory. "Compute" means to calculate. **Enumerate**, which means to count one by one, is most appropriate.
35.	B	"Quick, adequate response" should provide a clue here. What would be an appropriate punishment for "systematic bullies?" An **expulsion**, of course.
36.	B	"Though badly damaged" implies that the missing word should contrast our expectation. Damaged ancient writing is likely to be illegible. So, our prediction based on context should be "readable," or "understandable." **Decipherable**, which means able to be understood or decoded, is most appropriate.
37.	B	"Questioning" means raising questions. "Reasonable" means agreeable to reason. "Detailed" means focused on minutiae. "Break down into logical functions" is explained by "analysis." Therefore, an **analytical** mind is the correct description.
38.	B	"Material" means relating to a substance. "Mortal" means relating to death or belonging to this world. **Corporeal**, which means relating or having a body, aptly describes the type of human existence we are familiar with. Since the chief distinction between life and afterlife is the presence of a body, "material" and "mortal" are inadequate.

39.	C	"Optimize" means to make as useful or effective as possible. "Levitate" means to float onto air. "Elected" means to choose, especially by vote. **Elevate** means to raise to a higher position. In abstract meaning, it could mean to exalt, or hold high. Since we're looking to move the status up, **elevate** is most appropriate.
40.	B	"Diligent" meaning busy and focused on task. "Stringent" means rigorous or strict. "Dispassionate" means free from personal feeling or inclinations. Since "contrary" implies the opposite of the imperialists' expectation, **emphatically**, meaning passionately, is appropriate. The conquered population is expected to be angry at the conquerors, but the expectation was broken.

Contributors

Written and edited by the talented test prep professionals at

PaulAcademy is the publishing arm of one of the industry-leading test prep organizations in Asia. PaulAcademy is a dedicated test prep organization that has helped thousands of students to realize their potentials and achieve their dreams. As a leader in test prep & strategy development specializing in SAT, ACT and AP preparation, PaulAcademy teaches pragmatic problem-solving skills that will ultimately help students obtain successful academic results. PaulAcademy aims to spread its expert knowledge to students worldwide.

Editor-in-Chief
Paul Kim

Head of Publishing
Niles Bliss

Material Development & Editing
Taekjoon Kim
Hyunseung Yang

✔ Paul Academy

Email: books@paulacademy.net   Website: http://www.paulacademy.net

ISBN :